The Galveston Hurricane

The Galveston Hurricane

Kristine Brennan

CHELSEA HOUSE PUBLISHERS
Philadelphia

Frontispiece: The Galveston Hurricane of 1900 is arguably the worst natural disaster in United States history. In this photograph, Galveston residents stand among the ruins of their homes.

CHELSEA HOUSE PUBLISHERS

Editor in Chief Sally Cheney
Director of Production Kim Shinners
Creative Manager Takeshi Takahashi
Manufacturing Manager Diann Grasse

Staff for THE GALVESTON HURRICANE

Assistant Editor Susan Naab
Picture Researcher Sarah Bloom
Production Assistant Jaimie Winkler
Series Designer Takeshi Takahashi
Cover Designer Keith Trego
Layout 21st Century Publishing and Communications, Inc.

CH 6|20|02 ZZL

First Printing

1 3 5 7 9 8 6 4 2

The Chelsea House World Wide Web address is
http://www.chelseahouse.com

Library of Congress Cataloging-in-Publication Data

Brennan, Kristine, 1969–
     The Galveston hurricane / Kristine Brennan.
       p. cm. — (Great disasters, reforms and ramifications)
Summary: An account of the tragic Galveston hurricane of 1900 that claimed over six thousand lives.
Includes bibliographical references and index.
     ISBN 0-7910-6740-8 (hardcover : alk. paper)
   1. Galveston (Tex.)—History—20th century—Juvenile literature.
2. Hurricanes—Texas—Galveston—History—20th century—
Juvenile literature. 3. Floods—Texas—Galveston—History—
20th century—Juvenile literature. [1. Hurricanes—Texas—
Galveston. 2. Galveston (Tex.)] I. Title. II. Series.
F394.G2 B74 2002
976.4'139—dc21
                                   2002001417

Contents

GREAT DISASTERS
REFORMS and RAMIFICATIONS

Jill McCaffrey
National Chairman
Armed Forces Emergency Services
American Red Cross

Introduction

Disasters have always been a source of fascination and awe. Tales of a great flood that nearly wipes out all life are among humanity's oldest recorded stories, dating at least from the second millennium B.C., and they appear in cultures from the Middle East to the Arctic Circle to the southernmost tip of South America and the islands of Polynesia. Typically gods are at the center of these ancient disaster tales—which is perhaps not too surprising, given the fact that the tales originated during a time when human beings were at the mercy of natural forces they did not understand.

To a great extent, we still are at the mercy of nature, as anyone who reads the newspapers or watches nightly news broadcasts can attest.

Hurricanes, earthquakes, tornados, wildfires, and floods continue to exact a heavy toll in suffering and death, despite our considerable knowledge of the workings of the physical world. If science has offered only limited protection from the consequences of natural disasters, it has in no way diminished our fascination with them. Perhaps that's because the scale and power of natural disasters force us as individuals to confront our relatively insignificant place in the physical world and remind us of the fragility and transience of our lives. Perhaps it's because we can imagine ourselves in the midst of dire circumstances and wonder how we would respond. Perhaps it's because disasters seem to bring out the best and worst instincts of humanity: altruism and selfishness, courage and cowardice, generosity and greed.

As one of the national chairmen of the American Red Cross, a humanitarian organization that provides relief for victims of disasters, I have had the privilege of seeing some of humanity's best instincts. I have witnessed communities pulling together in the face of trauma; I have seen thousands of people answer the call to help total strangers in their time of need.

Of course, helping victims after a tragedy is not the only way, or even the best way, to deal with disaster. In many cases planning and preparation can minimize damage and loss of life—or even avoid a disaster entirely. For, as history repeatedly shows, many disasters are caused not by nature but by human folly, shortsightedness, and unethical conduct. For example, when a land developer wanted to create a lake for his exclusive resort club in Pennsylvania's Allegheny Mountains in 1880, he ignored expert warnings and cut corners in reconstructing an earthen dam. On May 31, 1889, the dam gave way, unleashing 20 million tons of water on the towns below. The Johnstown Flood, the deadliest in American history, claimed more than 2,200 lives. Greed and negligence would figure prominently in the Triangle Shirtwaist Company fire in 1911. Deplorable conditions in the garment sweatshop, along with a failure to give any thought to the safety of workers, led to the tragic deaths of 146 persons. Technology outstripped wisdom only a year later, when the designers of the luxury liner *Titanic* smugly declared their state-of-the-art ship "unsinkable," seeing no need to provide lifeboat capacity for everyone onboard. On the night of April 14, 1912, more than 1,500 passengers and crew paid for this hubris with their lives after the ship collided with an iceberg and sank. But human catastrophes aren't always the unforeseen consequences of carelessness or folly. In the 1940s the leaders of Nazi Germany purposefully and systematically set out to exterminate all Jews, along with Gypsies, homosexuals, the mentally ill, and other so-called undesirables. More recently terrorists have targeted random members of society, blowing up airplanes and buildings in an effort to advance their political agendas.

The books in the GREAT DISASTERS: REFORMS AND RAMIFICATIONS series examine these and other famous disasters, natural and human made. They explain the causes of the disasters, describe in detail how events unfolded, and paint vivid portraits of the people caught up in dangerous circumstances. But these books are more than just accounts of what happened to whom and why. For they place the disasters in historical perspective, showing how people's attitudes and actions changed and detailing the steps society took in the wake of each calamity. And in the end, the most important lesson we can learn from any disaster—as well as the most fitting tribute to those who suffered and died—is how to avoid a repeat in the future.

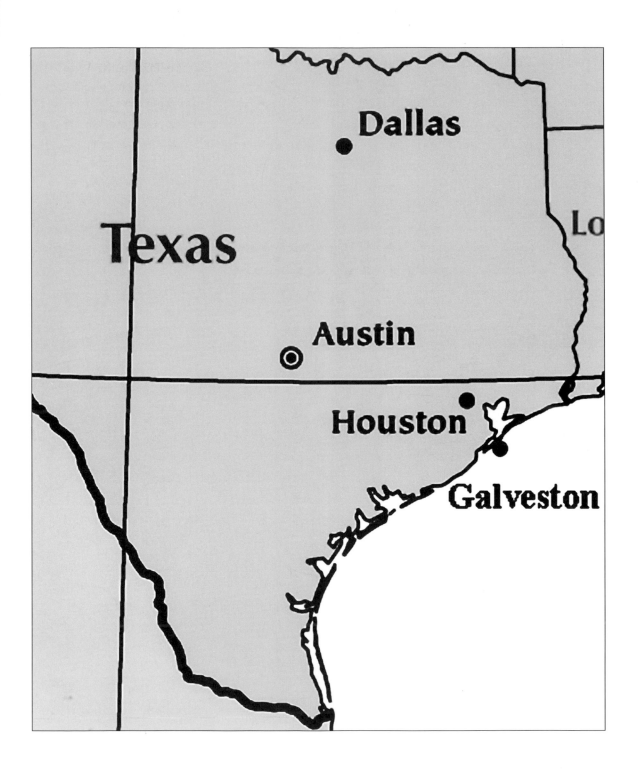

As shown in this map, the city of Galveston sits on a 32-mile sandbar two miles from the Texas coast. With Galveston Bay on one side and the Gulf of Mexico on the other, Galveston stood unprotected from the storm surge that claimed approximately 6,000 lives in September 1900.

Disaster Strikes the "Queen City of the Gulf"

On the night of September 8, 1900, a half-drowned Isaac Monroe Cline regained consciousness. He found himself adrift on a storm tide, wedged between pieces of lumber that had, until a short time ago, been a building. His own house had toppled into the current. A violent late-summer hurricane packing winds in excess of 100 miles per hour and driving rains forced water into Cline's eyes, nose, and mouth. Waters from the Gulf of Mexico to the east side of Galveston Island met with the waters of Galveston Bay to the west side, flooding beaches, streets, and buildings with cold, swirling salt water.

Where were Isaac Cline's wife, brother, and three little girls—with whom he had just been huddled in a bedroom on the second story of the family home? Isaac had fully expected to drown after the collapsing house dragged him underwater. Lightning flashes afforded him only intermittent glances of the bodies and debris floating all around him. As he searched for the rest of his family on the frothing waters of the storm, Isaac Monroe Cline's struggle for survival was only beginning.

His fight for life was just one among thousands transpiring at that moment, as the Galveston Hurricane whipsawed the small Texas barrier island from September 8 to 9, 1900. This storm took more lives than any other natural disaster in U.S. history. Estimates vary, but most accounts of the storm place the number of deaths in Galveston at about 6,000. Approximately one-third of the city's buildings ceased to exist by early Sunday, September 9.

The Galveston Hurricane did more than end thousands of lives; it also permanently altered the lives of those who survived it. Galveston's political landscape changed after the storm as surely as its streets had. Immediately after the hurricane, the dazed and tattered survivors were subject to martial law as they struggled to rebuild. Disposing of the numerous dead and removing the mountains of debris presented staggering challenges. The people of the island scraped by with help from donations from around the world and thanks to the administrative skills of Clara Barton, president of the American National Red Cross. After they had dealt with the worst horrors the storm had visited on Galveston, city leaders sought to protect the island from future hurricanes.

Galveston is a barrier island about two miles out from the Gulf coast of Texas. It is essentially a sandbar 32 miles long and between 1.5 and 3 miles in width at various points. The island and city were named in 1786 for Bernardo de Galvez, a Spanish governor, who, ironically, died without ever having seen Galveston. An explorer commissioned by Bernardo de Galvez named it in his honor. Galveston Island had been inhabited long before Spain laid claim to it, however. During the 1500s, the Karankawa tribe fished and camped on its beaches.

In 1817, a pirate baron name Jean Lafitte renamed the island Campeche and ran a thriving slave market in his adopted home base. Campeche literally went down in flames when Lafitte burned his gambling establishments and slave compound after being driven off Galveston Island for attacking an American ship. Texas did not officially become part of the United States until December 29, 1845: it became an independent republic, however, in 1836, after the American defeat of Mexico (which, since becoming independent of Spain, had control of Texas). Galveston Island served as an important U.S. naval stronghold during the war with Mexico for possession of Texas.

In 1836, a French-Canadian investor named Michel B. Menard purchased a seven square mile area from Texas to found the city of Galveston. No doubt, Galveston Island's deep natural harbor attracted Menard and his nine associates. They incorporated the city of Galveston in 1839. The harbor soon came to bustling life, with ships from around the world importing goods like coffee and bananas, and exporting cotton on a grand scale. Galveston was also an official point of entry into the United States, giving the city an ethnically diverse population and a rich labor pool.

The Union Blockade of Galveston Harbor from 1861 to 1862 during the Civil War put the brakes on the city's development. After the war, however, Galveston became the first city in Texas to achieve numerous milestones of modernization. Galveston was a shining

Galveston's naturally deep harbor made it a busy shipping center. During the Civil War, Union forces block -aded the harbor to cut off Confederate lines of supply. In January of 1863 Confederate ships surprised and captured the Union steamer *Harriet Lane* at Galveston Harbor.

city, resplendent with wealth and its attendant creature comforts. The city beat Houston in the race to become the first city in Texas equipped with electric lights (1883) and telephone service (1878).

Galveston was not only the first Texas city to have electric lights and telephone service; the island was also first to establish a post office, a military base (Fort Crockett), and grocery stores. Gary Carter writes that many of Galveston's first grocers made their own rules as they went along. "Merchants saw nothing wrong with overcharging for a bag of groceries, but by habit they threw in a free package of lemon drops."

In fact, many Galvestonians seemed to play by their own rules. The more adventurous would swim nude on

the beach late at night and into the wee hours of the morning. The most reckless indulged in gambling and visited prostitutes—both of which were readily available on the island.

Galveston at the turn of the twentieth century may have been the best of both worlds: a modern, well-appointed southern city that was still isolated from the rest of Texas. Here, people could try to live their dreams without too much fear of censure. Carter describes Galveston's slightly decadent climate as having "a sort of Toy Town mystique that suggested that life was a party that went on forever." Indeed, Galvestonians knew how to enjoy the finer things in life: the city boasted Texas's first jewelry store, and also the first golf course.

The University of Texas Medical Branch (the state's first medical college, founded in 1886 and still in existence today) kept widows with spare rooms in business as landladies, since the school attracted students from around the country. Galveston's culture was varied and vibrant, fueled by a large immigrant population and a sizeable (20% of the total population) black community. Leisure time in Galveston could mean taking in a concert, play, or opera. It might also just as easily mean watching bicycle races at the velodrome (bicycle race track) or visiting a beer garden.

Galveston's *wharves* infused the city with the income that fueled the island's vibrancy and life. The city was a premier exporter of cotton. Black and white dockworkers toiled together—albeit in separate labor unions. Certainly, Galveston's racial relations left much to be desired in the late nineteenth century, but the city viewed itself as open-minded, modern, and loaded with the best of everything. Erik Larson, author of *Isaac's Storm*, writes:

> Galveston was too pretty, too progressive, too prosperous —entirely too hopeful—to be true. Travelers arriving by ship saw the city as a silvery fairy kingdom that might just as suddenly disappear from sight, a very different portrait from that which would present itself in the last few weeks of September 1900, when inbound passengers smelled the pyres of burning corpses a hundred miles out to sea.

Broadway, also known as 25th Street, was Galveston's main thoroughfare, traversing the entire length of the city. The Strand (Avenue B) was known as the "Wall Street of the Southwest" because it was lined with grain and cotton brokers, stores, and financial institutions.

At a little less than nine feet above sea level, Broadway

was the highest point on the island in 1900. Galveston Island was all sand and low, marshy ground. The surf rushed into the streets during storms with an almost boring regularity. The predictability of this flooding may have contributed to thousands of deaths: after all, many islanders assumed the creeping tide that they observed early on Saturday, September 8, 1900 was just more of the same.

Galveston could have taken a page from the sad story of Indianola, once a thriving port city on Matagorda Bay, 150 miles from Galveston. In 1875, a hurricane had destroyed most of Indianola's structures and claimed 20 percent of its population. The residents rebuilt and restored Indianola to business as usual— until 1886. That year, a second hurricane sent water surging over the city. The fact that Indianola was built behind a small line of barrier islands that protected it to some small degree is a testament to the severity of both the first and second storms. The 1886 storm took an even greater toll on Indianola than the first one had, prompting survivors to abandon the town once and for all.

Just weeks after the final destruction of Indianola in 1886, a group of Galvestonians made plans to construct a protective wall around the city to spare it from the same fate. The group obtained the Texas government's approval to proceed, but then concern dissolved into complacency. Perhaps because the city's leaders feared scaring off potential businesses and vacationers by erecting a seawall, the project never got off the ground. Galveston did not take the tragedy of Indianola seriously enough until it was too late.

It was already too late for Galveston on Tuesday, September 5, 1900. That day a tropical disturbance was pummeling Cuba with wind and rain. Watercraft off

Florida in the Gulf of Mexico floundered in rough water. The U.S. Weather Bureau saw no reason to alarm the residents of the Gulf coast of Texas prematurely. Indeed, the head of the U.S. Weather Bureau discounted the warnings of Cuban forecasters who maintained that the storm passing over Cuba and Florida was indeed a hurricane—and that it would head for Texas. (After it happened, the U.S. Weather Bureau insisted that the Galveston Hurricane was an entirely different weather system, on the grounds that a cyclone couldn't possibly travel from Florida to Galveston).

The Galveston weather station, located at the top of the Levy Building at 23rd Street and Avenue D, was part of the U.S. Weather Bureau. At its helm was Isaac Monroe Cline. He had moved his family to Galveston from Abilene in 1889 to straighten out the island city's rag-tag weather station. A physician by training, Dr. Cline was a pioneer in the field of medical climatology, the study of how weather conditions affect the human body.

At the time of the storm, he and his wife, Cora May, had three daughters and were expecting a fourth child. The Clines lived at 2511 Avenue Q, which was three blocks from the beach on the Gulf side of Galveston. The house he lived in at the time of the storm had been built in 1896. Isaac believed he had made sure that his dwelling was engineered to withstand rough coastal weather. His younger brother and assistant, Joseph L. Cline, also lived in the house.

John Blagden, a third weather observer, was temporarily assigned to Galveston; his usual territory was Memphis, Tennessee. Blagden would have the dubious honor of riding out the hurricane in the weather station as it teetered precariously in the wind.

But neither of the Clines nor Blagden had any

idea what the "tropical disturbance" would mean to Galveston until it slammed into the city as a full-blown hurricane. On Friday, September 7, the men hoisted a red flag emblazoned with a black square atop the weather station; this flag was a signal warning Galveston of an impending storm. Although they knew that rough weather was on its way, they were unable to accurately estimate its magnitude. In fact, Isaac Cline later recalled that Friday, September 7, had been "an ideal day as far as weather was concerned, a calm before the storm."

How, then, did Isaac Cline find himself clinging to rubble in the violent, cold swells of a 15-foot storm tide a little more than 24 hours later—his lungs filled with water and his arms empty of his wife and children?

In the days prior to the disaster, Galveston's weather station discounted Cuban reports of a huge storm headed for the Texas coast and failed to warn residents of the coming hurricane. This illustration shows the staff of the "fact room" of a typical weather station in the late 1800s.

A Rude
Awakening

This lithograph shows the magnitude of destruction leveled on Galveston by the hurricane of September 8, 1900. The powerful storm surge fully engulfed the city, crushing homes to splinters and killing thousands of residents.

2

With most of Galveston still slumbering early on Saturday, September 8, Isaac Cline's concern about the coming storm mounted. He ventured onto the beach near his home at around 5:00 A.M. He noted that the barometer (an instrument used to determine the pressure of the atmosphere) was not dropping rapidly, as might be expected prior to a devastating storm. He estimated the wind to be blowing at 15 to 17 miles per hour. But Cline's attention was riveted to one minor detail as he looked at the apparently tranquil beach: although the wind was blowing offshore, the tide continued to rise against it. "The storm swells were increasing in manner and frequency and were building up a storm tide," he later wrote, "which told me as plainly as though it was a written message that great danger was approaching. Neither the barometer, nor the winds were telling me, but the storm tide was telling me to warn the people of the danger approaching."

In his autobiography, *Storms, Floods, and Sunshine*, Isaac Cline states that he was sufficiently alarmed by the beginnings of the storm tide to return on his horse-drawn cart and drive the length of the beach. He wrote:

> I warned the people that great danger threatened them, and advised some 6,000 persons, from the interior of the State, who were summering along the beach to go home immediately. I warned persons residing within three blocks of the beach to move to the higher portions of the city, that their houses would be undermined by the ebb and flow of the increasing storm tide and would be washed away.

Cline gave himself ample credit for his efforts. "Some 6,000 lives were saved by my advice and warnings," he later claimed. But Erik Larson says that no other accounts of the storm mention Isaac Cline riding along the shoreline and warning beachgoers.

If he did in fact hitch up his horse and warn the public, Isaac Cline did so in direct defiance of the U.S. Weather Bureau. Even though Cline's warning was only verbal, the Weather Bureau's policy was that only its central office in Washington, D.C. could issue hurricane warnings. After the storm, however, Willis Moore, chief of the U.S. Weather Bureau, was willing to both overlook Isaac's transgression and to believe his claims of heroism. Moore praised Cline as "one of the heroic spirits of that awful Saturday."

It was Isaac Cline's younger brother and assistant weather observer Joseph who awoke on Saturday morning before dawn and alerted Isaac to the surf lapping in the yard. Joseph Cline believed that Isaac should call for an evacuation of Galveston. Isaac was the expert, though, and Joseph, his subordinate. Isaac's claims of spreading the word early Saturday not withstanding, most people in Galveston went about their business and scarcely noticed the rising water until the afternoon—when the fate of many people was already sealed. It is possible that the Cline brothers' disagreement about how to handle the storm and the disastrous results of Isaac's miscalculation led to their eventual estrangement from one another after the Galveston Hurricane.

Prior to this cataclysmic storm, which would knock his house into the sea, Isaac Monroe Cline did not believe Galveston was vulnerable to severe hurricanes. "The opinion held by some who are unacquainted with the actual conditions of things, that Galveston will at some time be seriously damaged by some disturbance" he had written in the *Galveston News* in 1891, "is simply an absurd delusion."

Dr. Cline's assertion would only seem outrageous when read through the lens of clear-eyed hindsight. Nobody in America knew much about hurricanes in his day, although this didn't stop forecasters from trying to predict their behavior. A hurricane is a tropical cyclone with winds exceeding 74 miles per hour, that circulate around a center of low atmospheric pressure (the eye) in a counterclockwise direction in the Northern Hemisphere. (The winds of a cyclone blow clockwise in the Southern Hemisphere.) They form from groups of thunderstorms over warm ocean waters. These blocks of thunderstorms require water vapor from warm ocean waters and warm, humid air to mature into hurricanes.

As thunderstorms start grouping together, they form a tropical depression, a precursor to a hurricane. The wind starts blowing between 23-29 miles per hour in a counterclockwise direction at this point. The winds blow counterclockwise because of the earth's rotation; the phenomenon is known as the *Coriolis effect*. The term "depression" comes from a point of low atmospheric pressure at the center of this group of storms. At this early stage, however, the cyclone does not have too much noticeable rotation. As the winds gain speed from the moisture of the warm surface water, the cyclone intensifies into a tropical storm (winds 39-73 miles per hour). As cool, more organized and faster winds push warm, vapor-saturated air upward, a counterclockwise whirlpool of air forms around a center of low pressure about 15-20 miles in diameter. Even if a cyclone dissipates before wind speeds increase to hurricane force (74 miles per hour or more), a tropical storm can be very dangerous when it makes landfall because the heavy rains it brings can cause floods and mudslides.

Hurricanes also carry heavy rains, but rain is not their deadliest weapon. The greatest danger to life and property posed by a hurricane is its storm surge. Storm surge is the water pushed onshore by a hurricane's powerful rotating winds. Storm tide is the total height of water flooding a coastal area; it is the combination of storm surge and the regular tide. Many of the houses destroyed during the Galveston Hurricane of 1900 would have withstood the winds alone: it was repeated battering by the storm tide that toppled them into the sea.

With its warm Gulf waters, Galveston Island—just a sandbar, really—was a prime breeding ground for hurricanes during the month of September. Cuban meteorologists knew the cyclone that had passed over Cuba and Florida on September 5 was gaining in strength and speed—and that it was headed west to

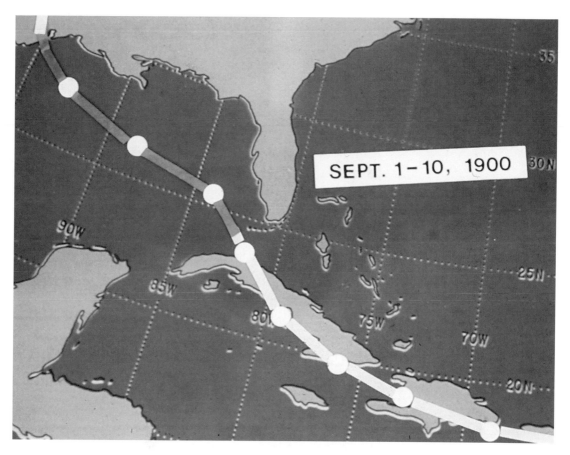

SEPT. 1-10, 1900

Texas. American forecasters, on the other hand, were convinced that a cyclone could only travel north: they predicted that the cyclone would affect the Mid-Atlantic states and leave Texas with little more than blustery rain.

The U.S. Weather Bureau did have a station in Cuba that operated under the authority of the War Department, but the forecasters there were firmly convinced that the hurricane could not possibly hit Galveston. Furthermore, they thought that Cuban meteorologists like those at Havana's Belen Observatory were unnecessarily alarmist in their warnings. In August of 1900, the U.S. government had instituted a ban on Cuban weather cables, though they were often

This map shows the track of the Galveston Hurricane from September 1-10, 1900 as it crossed the islands of the Caribbean, strengthened in the Gulf of Mexico, and hit Galveston with full force.

superior to forecasts from the U. S. Weather Bureau. So completely did America miss out on the benefits of Cuban meteorology that after the Galveston Hurricane had laid waste to a large segment of Texas, U.S. Weather Bureau officials refused to believe that this storm was the same one that had passed over Cuba and Florida. They stubbornly insisted that it was an entirely separate cyclone!

It was against this backdrop of ignorance and denial that Dr. Cline began to feel uneasy on September 8. While Isaac made his alleged ride along the beach, Joseph Cline and John Blagden manned the phones at the weather station.

Not everyone in the general public was unaware of the seriousness of the situation before noon on September 8, though. An anonymous letter written by a woman to her lover during the storm begins with a description of the John Sealy Hospital—where she worked— surrounded by encroaching water that morning. "Have my hands full quieting nervous, hysterical women," she noted.

For most people, however, it still seemed like a harmless rainy Saturday in Galveston. Some people welcomed the rain as a respite from the searing heat and humidity that had been boiling them alive that summer. As for the water that had begun flowing into the streets as people headed out to their jobs (Saturday was a workday at this time), these so-called "overflows" were not unusual because of the island's low elevation.

If most humans didn't sense the storm's latent menace, perhaps some animals did. Some survivors said that their pets and livestock seemed especially skittish that day, even before their human caretakers understood the true extent of the danger they faced. Journalist Steve Olafson opened a story in the August 28, 2000 edition of the *Houston Chronicle* with this eerie animal story to commemorate the 100-year anniversary of the hurricane:

> On the morning of Saturday, Sept. 8, 1900, a horse without rider or saddle galloped through the rain-swept streets of Galveston.
>
> Spooked by a fast-closing storm, the horse raced north on 12th Street, then turned east on Sealy, where it found a swinging gate and a front door left open by someone who had walked to the corner to look to the surging Gulf of Mexico.
>
> The horse turned into the yard, passed through the house's open door and climbed the stairs to the second floor.
>
> It remained there for three days.

Even if Isaac Monroe Cline had wanted to order an evacuation based on Joseph's fearful hunch, it was already too late by midmorning. The last train to make it out of Galveston left at 9:00 A.M; by noon, the station stopped selling tickets. The tide rose higher in the streets and the rain fell. A trainload of unfortunate souls made it into the doomed city from Houston at around 1:00 P.M. As they approached, they needed to switch trains because of flooding. The fresh train crawled into Galveston as workers walked alongside it, plucking wind-driven debris from the track.

The wind continued to pick up speed. The rain gauge and the *anenometer* (wind speed gauge) blew away from the Galveston weather station that afternoon. Before it was all over, the wind howled well in excess of 100 miles per hour. During lunchtime at Ritter's Café, a gust blew the roof off the building. Printing presses rained down from the print shop above the café onto the diners below. Five patrons died: five more were severely injured. A waiter who ran to fetch a doctor drowned in the streets of

Galveston. Although some cheerfully oblivious children still plunged and waded in the water that was now flowing deeply in their yards, their mothers knew that the situation was getting serious. So did David Benjamin, a businessman who had arrived in Galveston on that last train from Houston. He got off the train and headed for a meeting but the waist-high and deeper water in the street and the intense winds turned him back towards the station. There, he saw something that drove the gravity of the storm home to him: a child's lifeless body floated into the train station.

Many people sought shelter in public buildings or in the sturdiest homes in their neighborhoods. Others elected to stay put, sometimes with disastrous results. Judson Palmer joked with his coworkers about his wife's fearfulness—until he returned home from his job as a clerk at the YMCA to find his backyard flooded and water flowing into the house. His wife, Mae, urged him to take her and their little boy to the YMCA building to wait out the storm. Judson Palmer insisted on staying home. A few hours later, the water would ambush all three Palmers as they huddled in an upstairs bathtub. When the storm surge flooded over Judson Palmer's head, he lost his grip on his wife and son. He surfaced alone and gasping in the swirling tide

All around the city, wide-eyed children watched their parents chop holes into the upstairs floors of their houses. Homeowners reasoned that if they permitted a small amount of floodwater to flow into the upper level of their homes, then the weight of the water would help stabilize the houses and prevent them from being swept away. The waters of the Gulf and Galveston Bay met over the island between 3:00 and 5:00 P.M. Saturday. Galveston was now completely underwater, with the storm tide approximately eight feet deep. The water in the streets was

deeper or shallower, depending upon the elevation of a given area and the amount of debris displacing the flood-water. The storm tide was not a direct result of the rain, although this contributed to the flooding. Instead, the winds of the hurricane were so powerful that they acted like a giant shovel, pushing water over the island in addition to the regular tides.

At around 3:30 P.M., Isaac Cline drafted a telegram warning the Washington, D.C., headquarters of the Weather Bureau that Galveston was expecting a cata-strophic storm. He wrote that he anticipated a large loss of life and a pressing need for aid in the aftermath. He dispatched his brother Joseph to the telegraph office. Joseph Cline's plodding journey through the deep water led him to the telephone exchange after he discovered that the telegraph lines were already out of commission. He talked the telephone operator into giving him the last working line in town so that he could call Houston's

As this dramatic photo shows, the force of the tidal surge toppled houses like toys, plowing one house into another.

Western Union office and send the telegraph through them. Joseph barely managed to transmit Isaac's message before that last telephone line went out of service, too.

When Isaac Cline learned that Galveston was now totally isolated from the rest of the world, he struck out for home and his wife and daughters. He wrote in his autobiography:

> Having worked for the public ceaselessly from 5 A.M. until 3:30 P.M. and with no possibility of being able to further serve the populace, I waded nearly two miles to my home through water, often above my waist. Hurricane winds were driving timbers and slates through the air every where [sic] around me, splitting the paling and weather boarding of houses into splinters, and roofs of buildings were flying through the air.

Father Kirwin, a priest at the Galveston Cathedral, was watching the monstrous storm from inside the parochial house with Bishop Gallagher of the Archdiocese of Galveston and several other priests. The massive bell that called them to prayer crashed to the street. As a panicked horse charged through the rain towards the parochial house, a chunk of flying debris knocked the life out of it. "Prepare these priests for death," the bishop instructed Father Kirwin, indicating the others.

Everyday objects became dangerous missiles out on the street. According to author Erik Larson, "Decapitations occurred. Long splinters of wood pierced limbs and eyes." Those who survived terrifying walks home in the storm devised some novel methods of protecting themselves. Salesman Arnold Wolfram had 20 perilous blocks to go. He remembered the new shoes he was carrying, and got an idea. "Standing in the shelter of a doorway," he later recalled, "I unwrapped my shoes, tied them together and fastened them to my head." Wolfram rescued a young boy from spiraling to his death down a storm drain, and convinced the boy to use his shoes as a makeshift helmet, too.

They did not make it to Wolfram's house. Instead, they weathered the storm clinging together in a tree, until a piece of wood lodged in the tree and formed a plank leading to the entrance of a house. Arnold Wolfram's young friend never forgot his rescuer: the two remained in contact for many years after the hurricane.

Weather observer John Blagden was actually fortunate in that he did not try to return home. He spent a harrowing Saturday night in the weather station on top of the swaying Levy Building. But when Blagden wrote his family to assure them he had survived unhurt, he also mentioned that the entire family with whom he was lodging had perished in the storm.

Dr. Cline arrived home to find his house filled with some 50 refugees of the storm in addition to his wife, daughters, and brother. His guests included the home's builder and his family. They were there when the storm reached its peak between 6:00 and 8:00 P.M. According to some accounts, the water rose four feet in as many seconds sometime after seven o'clock. The storm's eye wall was over Galveston, packing the highest winds and heaviest rains of the entire hurricane. The driving winds pushed more water over the island; the storm tide reached depths of over 15 feet with remarkable rapidity. Isaac Monroe Cline's house fell over when a loose railroad trestle rammed into it.

As he was pulled underwater with his collapsing house, Cline was certain that he would drown. The next morning would bring untold sorrows as well as numerous stories of survival every bit as miraculous as his.

Survivors and Victims

3

When Isaac Cline had come home, he found his family on the second floor of his house; the first floor was flooded. Isaac joined his six-year-old "baby," Esther, and his wife, Cora, who lay in bed. The two older Cline daughters, Allie May and Rosemary, were near a window with their "Uncle Joe." The house withstood the storm until a long railroad trestle rammed into it, knocking it off of its foundation. Joseph Cline managed to grab his two older nieces and escape through a window with them. The collapsed walls dragged Isaac underwater: he was certain he was dying.

Isaac came to, wedged between floating timbers but very much alive. The flashing lightning revealed a small figure bobbing in the current: little Esther. She was scared, but not seriously hurt. As Isaac held his youngest daughter to his chest and tried to stay afloat, he was blessed yet again by the sight of his two older girls. Allie May and Rosemary were drifting on a piece of wreckage with Joseph. They made room for Isaac and Esther to join them. The Cline brothers shielded Esther, Rosemary, and Allie May from debris driven hard enough by the current to cause serious injuries. Several times, the wreckage pummeled their makeshift raft so fiercely that Isaac and Joseph fell into the cold floodwaters and then struggled back to the three girls.

Joseph's dog swam through the storm to his family at one point. But this small miracle was short-lived: the dog plunged back into the salty water although Joseph called to him pleadingly. Joseph Cline may have lost his dog in the hurricane, but he also had the good fortune to rescue a child from the wild and deadly water. When he saw a little girl flailing in the current, he assumed that it was Esther fallen overboard and plucked her to safety. Then, he turned to see Esther already safe and sound aboard the raft.

So who was this child he had grabbed from the swirling waters? The little girl told the Clines that she was four years old, and that she was in Galveston visiting relatives with her mother when the storm struck. She remained in the care of another Galveston family until her relatives could be found. By another stroke of luck, Joseph happened to overhear a father asking after his lost little girl as he waited in line at a store two weeks after the storm. Joseph astutely realized that the little girl the father sought was the one he had rescued. He completed the circle of good fortune he had begun by leading the frantic father to his waiting daughter.

But Joseph, the little motherless girl, Isaac and his three daughters would all have to ride out the rest of the storm before they could even contemplate any future happiness. The driving rain made it impossible for them to keep their eyes open for too long. The wind propelled wreckage through the air and over the turbulent water with enough force to fracture skulls and impale limbs.

The Clines' wooden lifeboat ran aground in a yard at 28th and P around midnight. Their perilous journey had started at approximately 8:30 P.M., sweeping them out to sea and then back to the submerged island again. The storm tide was still at its peak at about that time. The strong winds and the broken buildings and debris displaced water, making the tide fluctuate violently. Water levels on the island ranged from approximately 10.5 feet to nearly 16 feet, depending upon the ground's elevation.

By midnight, the water was receding. Battered and bruised, the bedraggled father, uncle, and children spent the remainder of the night as guests of a family at 28th and P. Although Isaac's three girls had cried for their mother earlier, now they were too exhausted to stay awake. Dr. Cline could not escape the conclusion that Cora was dead. When the Clines found her body several weeks later, they would discover that she had died pinned beneath the very wreckage that had kept her family afloat during the storm.

Isaac and Joseph agreed to pay for the care of the little girl they had scooped from the water, but the family that hosted the Clines after the storm housed her. By the time Isaac and his children had found and buried Cora's remains (she was not burned), the little girl who had survived the tempest with them would be reunited with her jubilant father.

Louisa and August Rollfing and their children had a happy reunion of their own right after the worst of hurricane. Their family survived the storm intact despite August's refusal to come home when storm was intensifying on Saturday. He was a painter who had insisted on going to work on the morning of September 8. His wife Louisa Rollfing gradually came to suspect that the rain and the flooded streets were omens of far worse things to come. Over thirty years after the Galveston Hurricane, Mrs. Rollfing recalled that nobody thought much of the flooded city streets at first. "For a while even ladies were wading in the water," she wrote, "thinking it was *fun*." Soon, buildings on the beach were falling into the sea. Louisa Rollfing sent her son, August, Jr., to fetch his father from work so that the Rollfings could evacuate their house together. Little August came home alone. At noon, the elder August showed up for lunch. "I hadn't even thought about cooking, so we both were mad," Louisa wrote. Mr. Rollfing insisted on going back to town to pay his work crew—despite the fact that water was already seeping under their door.

This was the last straw for Louisa Rollfing. She demanded that August send a horse and buggy to take her, little August, and their daughters Helen and Atlanta to her mother-in-law's house further inland. He went back to town and waited for employees who never showed: they had sense enough not to venture out in the treacherous storm, even though August had their money.

One prudent thing that August did was to send a buggy to collect Louisa and his children. Mrs. Rollfing remembered that rushing waters, high winds, and downed electrical wires made it impossible for the buggy to reach her mother-in-law's home. The driver took them to her sister-in-law's house, instead. There, Louisa and her children nervously waited out the storm with her relatives and their neighbors. The heard the kitchen break off of the house and felt the foundation move. Miraculously, midnight came and everyone in the house was still alive.

But where was August? To Louisa Rollfing's amazement and relief, he literally flopped into his sister's house early on the morning of September 9, "more dead than alive." He had given up on waiting for his workers the previous afternoon, and spent the night wading, swimming, and struggling as he looked for his wife and children.

Judson Palmer, secretary of the Galveston YMCA, was less fortunate than August Rollfing. Like Rollfing, he had refused to listen to his wife's worries as salt water crept into the Palmer family's yard. Mae Palmer wanted Judson to take her and their young son, Lee, to the YMCA with him for the duration of the storm. Mr. Palmer refused to leave his house.

The height of the storm found the Palmers clinging together in an upstairs bathtub. The wind howled through the house, tearing it apart. Author Erik Larson describes how the storm cost Judson Palmer his wife and only son:

> The roof stood up and fell upon the family. They went under the water together. Palmer came up alone. He had swallowed a great volume of water. He saw nothing of Lee or Mae.

For parents who had more than one child, the storm presented multiple opportunities for indescribable grief.

The hurricane's destructive force was perhaps worst at the water's edge, where the storm surge swept houses and ships aside like leaves. Survivors told harrowing tales of clinging all night to debris before the gale subsided.

This case study appears in Nathan C. Greene's compilation, *Story of the 1900 Galveston Hurricane*:

> Mr. McIlhenny was rescued from the flood, but completely exhausted. He says the water came up so rapidly that he and his family sought safety upon the roof. He had his son Haven in his arms and the other children were strapped together. It was not long before a heavy piece of timber struck Haven, killing him. He then took up young Rice, and while he had him in his arms he was twice washed off the roof, and in this way young Rice was drowned.

The storm would also take Mr. McIlhenny's wife from him.

Those who managed to survive the storm were resourceful or just plain lucky. There were also some who were a little of both, though, and they selflessly saved the lives of others. Daniel Ransom was a black man who lived in a house on Galveston's Gulf coast. When his home finally buckled into the rising tide, he swam to safety. Then, from approximately 4:00 P.M. to 6:30 P.M., Ransom whisked some 45 people out of the water and led them inland to shelter.

All over the island, people sought dependable shelters. Some neighbors simply squeezed into the sturdiest-looking house on their block; others gathered in public places. St. Mary's University was one of those places. So was St. Mary's Infirmary, where hundreds of scared refugees crowded in with the sick and the injured.

Although Charles Law, a traveling salesman, wrote to his wife in Georgia that "several thousand people" sought safety in the grand Tremont Hotel (which today stands half a block from its old location as the Tremont House), contemporary estimates place the number at one thousand or less. But a thousand wet, frightened refugees in addition to the hotel's approximately 200 paying guests that night made for very tight quarters. "We were all huddled up in the hall ways [sic], as we could not go into the rooms as the windows were blown through and the plastering in the rooms were all blown down," Law wrote. Although the roof blew off of the Tremont, it was still one of the safer places to wait out the storm.

Some stranded railroad travelers took shelter at Union Station. It was here, according to businessman David Benjamin, that people realized that the storm was serious "when the body of a child floated into the station."

Fewer than half of those huddled in Isaac Cline's supposedly storm-resistant house survived. But one of the saddest stories of that terrible night came from St. Mary's Orphans' Asylum, located three miles outside of the city on the island's west coast. Ten Sisters of Charity of the Incarnate Word cared for 93 children there. As the hurricane worsened, the nuns evacuated the boys' dormitory and herded the orphans into the newer girls' dorm. As the boys' quarters noisily broke apart in the surging tide, everyone fled to the top level of the girls' dorm. The nuns tried to comfort and distract the children by leading them in the singing of hymns.

Then the girls' building began to creak and groan in the storm tide. "The storm advanced through the building quickly and systematically," wrote Erik Larson in *Isaac's Storm,* "as if hunting the children." Still leading the children in song, the nuns used lengths of clothesline to tether the younger ones to their own waists. When the waters finally knocked the girls' quarters down, all of the nuns and ninety of the children perished. Only three older boys escaped from the collapsing building and managed to ride out the storm on floating debris. The boys had not been tied to the other children and the nuns. Therefore, they did not become entangled in the wreckage when the girls' dormitory fell. When one of the drowned nuns was found, she was holding fast to two small children. Perhaps she was keeping a promise to hold them fast no matter what happened.

Not only would Father Kirwin survive the hurricane, he would go out to the beach not long afterward to look for any trace of the orphanage. He saw nothing to suggest that a building had ever been there. Two miles from the site, however, Father Kirwin did find a donation box that had been inside St. Mary's Orphans' Asylum.

In a twist of bitter irony, the box still bore the slogan, "Remember the Orphans."

On Friday, September 8, 2000, the Sisters of Charity order of nuns staged a ceremony to commemorate the valiant nuns and innocent children lost to the storm a century earlier. They sang hymns and placed a wreath on the beach where the orphanage once stood.

While children and their caretakers were dying tragically at St. Mary's orphanage, four new babies were being born in the sturdy Ursuline Convent, a huge walled structure in town that covered four city blocks. The nuns there hosted about 1000 hurricane victims on September 8. Some people floated in through the windows. All 400 people who huddled in Galveston's city hall building that Saturday night also lived to see Sunday morning.

Many of these survivors reported that between 6:00 and 8:00 P.M., the water abruptly rose several feet throughout the city—at about the same time as the center (eye) of the hurricane is thought to have passed over Galveston and the *eye wall* was above the island city. Isaac Cline later disagreed. "There was no sudden, extraordinary rise in the water with the passage of the center of the cyclone, and claims made to that effect by some in after years are incorrect," he insisted in his 1945 autobiography, *Storms, Floods and Sunshine*.

Whenever the water reached its peak, there was no disputing the devastation it left in its wake. Sunday, September 9, 1900, greeted many people still clinging to trees, towers, or whatever else had remained above water with sunny, rose-colored skies. It looked as if nothing so sinister as the Galveston Hurricane could ever have taken place.

But it had. Survivors saw bodies dangling from trees. Some of these victims had become tangled in the branches and drowned; others had been bitten by venomous snakes as they took refuge in the trees. Those who hadn't yet seen such grisly sights, like Galveston's police chief Ed Ketchum, took a first glance out their windows and guessed that perhaps four or five people had probably drowned overnight. The first estimates city leaders made of lives lost hovered around 500. The loss of 500 lives was bad enough to imagine: the worst was yet to come as people discovered the actual death toll. As the first dazed and half-naked survivors began wandering around what remained of their city—stepping over bodies as they went—their ordeal was just beginning.

In a touching ceremony, one hundred years after the hurricane, the Ursuline Chapel bell rings in memory of those who died when St. Mary's orphanage was destroyed.

The morning after the storm, the skies cleared and temperatures rose, providing an eerie contrast to the mass destruction in the streets of Galveston. What had been a thriving array of shops, saloons, and businesses was now an expanse of rubble.

Horror and Hope

Although many of the great storm's survivors were soaked to the bone and stripped naked by the fast, churning water, they would not be cold for long. Sunday, September 9, 1900, dawned beautiful and bright. The temperature soon soared. Unfathomable human suffering and horror unfolded beneath eerily peaceful skies. Gary Cartwright describes the horrible pleas for help that greeted the ears of stunned survivors as they passed mounds of wreckage:

> They heard faint cries from people buried alive. At first, their impulse was to attempt rescues . . . but it was hopeless. No human effort could alter the inevitable or limit the final suffering of those who were trapped and waiting to die.

Charles Law, the Georgia salesman who stayed in the Tremont Hotel on the night of the storm, wrote his wife that the weather was "fearful hot" in the days following the hurricane. He estimated the temperature to be "98° to 99°."

People wandered the streets half-naked, cut and bruised by flying debris. The bright light of morning revealed just how much of the city was reduced to rubble. Downtown Galveston had been a modern, bustling collection of shops, saloons, and businesses just 24 hours earlier; now, it was a wasteland of broken glass, collapsed buildings, and the bloated, drowned bodies of people and livestock. Charles Law described the horror of what he saw in his letter to his wife:

> On Sunday morning after the storm was all over I went out into the streets and saw the most horrible sights that you can ever imagine. I gazed upon dead bodies lying here and there. The houses all blown into pieces; women men and children all walking the streets in a weak condition with bleeding heads and bodies and feet all torn to pieces with glass where they had been treading through the debris of fallen building[s]. And when I got to the gulf and bay coast I saw *hundreds* of houses all destroyed with dead bodies all lying in the ruins, little babies in their mothers [sic.] arms.

Although corpses lay in plain sight all around Galveston, the survivors still had no idea just how many souls the hurricane had claimed. This is because many more bodies remained hidden beneath the huge mountains of debris that now dotted the city. One of the biggest mounds was some 10 yards tall and three miles long. This tangled monument to the hurricane's power was located south of Broadway.

Not only did it conceal numerous human bodies and animal carcasses; it also interfered with the drainage of floodwater because it was so big. All four bridges connecting Galveston to mainland Texas were too severely damaged for safe passage.

The stagnating water trapped by debris, the bodies of storm victims, and the hot Galveston sun posed a health hazard to the living. The city's water tower was destroyed, leaving most people without potable water. Telephone and telegraph wires were down. All four bridges to mainland Texas (three rail bridges and one for wagon traffic) were also destroyed, effectively cutting off Galveston from the rest of the world—and much-needed aid.

Almost nobody left alive in Galveston escaped the grief of losing at least one relative or friend. Still, few who lived to tell the tale could remember hearing much weeping right after the storm. "The people of Galveston are stunned with the merciful bewilderment which nature always sends at such a time of sorrow," wrote Winifred Black, a reporter from the *New York Journal* who arrived during the first days of the recovery effort.

On Sunday morning, wagonloads of the dead—hastily covered up with heavy cloth—started arriving at a warehouse on the Strand, formerly the commercial hub of the city. Author Erik Larson likens this temporary morgue to bustling marketplace. "Men and women moved intently among the rows as if hunting bargains at a public market," he wrote. "Many bodies were uncovered, others lay under sheets and blankets, which survivors peeled back to expose the faces underneath.

People had some difficulty identifying their lost loved ones by simply peering into the faces of the dead. Many corpses were swollen beyond recognition from prolonged immersion in the water, or mangled by injuries sustained from flying debris. Some survivors found their dead kin because they recognized a distinguishing piece of jewelry (Dr. Cline eventually identified his wife Cora by her engagement ring.) or clothing.

The jewelry on victims' bodies gave rise to ugly rumors of widespread looting from the dead. Stories began to circulate about people stealing rings by amputating fingers from corpses, for example. Years after the storm, many people recalled seeing looters shot for such heinous deeds. Isaac Cline claimed that some 1000 "ghouls" were shot before Galveston's ordeal was over. Black people constituted some 20% of Galveston's total population and coexisted with whites in relative harmony before the storm. Unfortunately, virtually all of the stories of looting concerned blacks stealing from white victims. Journalists like Winifred Black did not help matters. This reference to an alleged black looter appeared in her description of Galveston in the wake of the hurricane:

> A young man well known in the city shot and killed a Negro who was cutting the ears from a dead woman's head to get her earrings out. The Negro lay in the street like a dead dog, and not even the members of his own race would give him the tribute of a kindly look.

To this day, there is no concrete proof that looting from corpses occurred after the Galveston Hurricane. John Blagden, the substitute weatherman who lived through the storm in the weather station atop the Levy Building, wrote to his family that four or five looters were allegedly shot in a single day. But he also cautioned that the story was unconfirmed: "I do not know how true it is for all kind of rumors are afloat and many of them are false." The sheer number of such

rumors may reflect the racial prejudices many white Galvestonians harbored at the dawn of the twentieth century. Racial prejudice would rear its ugly head numerous times as Galveston struggled to rebuild. Galveston's black population would find itself shut out of leadership roles during the city's recovery. At the same time, black workers often got stuck with the most odious jobs.

The prompt disposal of so many bodies in the summery heat promised to be the most disturbing task of all. In his book, *Galveston: a History of the Island*, Gary Cartwright describes "sewers plugged with vegetable, animal, and human remains," making safe water a precious commodity that most islanders didn't have. Even in the houses left standing, everything—furniture, clothing, blankets—was covered with putrid, slimy silt. The chaos left by the storm made swift and decisive action imperative, so that the maze

Locating, identifying and disposing of bodies was a monumental task for Galveston residents. To prevent the spread of disease from rotting corpses, a makeshift morgue was set up, and many bodies were hurriedly carted away for burial or cremation.

of bodies and debris covering the city would not contribute to disease among the survivors.

Galveston's surviving leaders were already swinging into action at 10:00 A.M. on Sunday, September 9. They met to determine how to cope with the previous night's disaster. It would not be easy. All telegraph and telephone lines were down; all the bridges connecting Galveston to the Texas mainland were down, too. The first order of business was to somehow alert the rest of the world to the devastation of Galveston.

The group worked fast; by 11:00 A.M., a party of six men was already on its way out of Galveston. The men managed to find a seaworthy steamboat, the *Pherabe*, and cross Galveston Bay to mainland Texas. From there, the messengers improvised, traveling by railroad handcar and then talking their way onto a passenger train to reach Houston. At 3:00 A.M. on Monday, September 10, they placed a telephone call to Texas governor Joseph Sayers and U.S. president William McKinley. President McKinley pledged federal aid to Governor Sayers to mitigate the effects of the storm.

Those left on the island could ill afford to wait idly for supplies and relief workers to come to them. At 2:00 P.M. on September 9—just a few hours after the party bound for Houston had departed—Galveston Mayor Walter C. Jones called a meeting of hurricane survivors at what was left of the Tremont Hotel. That first meeting of survivors marked the birth of the Central Relief Committee (CRC), a grassroots organization dedicated to rebuilding Galveston after the storm. Mayor Jones also declared that Galveston was under martial law. He deputized ordinary private citizens (all white men). These newly deputized men were empowered to force all able-bodied men to help in the recovery effort. They also had the authority to shoot looters on sight, if necessary.

The Central Relief Committee's most pressing problem was the sanitary disposal of so many corpses. Father Kirwin of the Galveston Cathedral did his best to assist those men compelled to pick up the bodies. He even went against his usual strict code of conduct and handed out alcoholic "stimulants" to the workers to take some of the sickening edge off of this horrible task. "I am a strong temperance man," Father Kirwin later said. "I pledge the children to total abstinence [from alcohol] at communion, but I went to the men who were handling those bodies and I gave them whiskey. It had to be done."

The burial division of the CRC was responsible for setting up the makeshift morgue on the Strand between 21st and 22nd streets. There, the city's elite lay touching elbows with Galveston's poorest in death. There was no time for individual funerals, and many of the dead were never identified. Many bereaved families would have to settle for framed certificates on their walls to memorialize their loved ones.

Although blacks and whites had taken refuge from the hurricane together in many cases, white Galvestonians' negative perception of their black neighbors returned as soon as the storm tide receded into the sea. All of Galveston's temporary deputies were white; there were no blacks on the CRC, either. Denied positions of authority, black people were assigned the most horrific tasks of the recovery effort. Some 50 black men— rounded up at gunpoint—did the distasteful, strenuous job of loading the dead onto barges on Monday night. Early Tuesday morning, these workers tossed some 700 bodies into the Gulf of Mexico. Many of the corpses had weights tied to them to prevent them from resurfacing. The bodies washed back onto Galveston's Gulf coast, anyway.

Having failed to bury bodies at sea, the CRC had two grim alternatives: immediate burial wherever bodies were found or mass cremations. There were so many bodies and the weather was so hot that burial was not practical. Galveston soon looked like it was on fire when viewed from a distance. Funereal pyres burned for weeks on end. The sickening smells of burning flesh, hair, and clothing filled the air well into November. Groups of workers called "dead gangs" were in charge of the cremations. The smell was so bad and the work so emotionally upsetting that the dead gangs only worked half-hour shifts.

Philip Gordie Tipp, 18 years old, supervised a dead gang that cremated more than 500 bodies in one pit. The awfulness of the experience stayed with him into old age. "It was the late part of November," he later recalled, "and I had done so much burning and so much work that I just gave out. I was sick for a long time. I can still smell the dead, and the burning bodies, like burnt sugar."

As unimaginable as it seems, people learned to go about their business as bodies burned around the city. They grew accustomed to the smell that Tipp described. But the horror of the cremations lingered in the memories of many. Emma Beal, who was a child at the time of the storm, recalled her reaction to the cremations during a 1972 interview:

> I stood out there and watched them burn some bodies. It was right up across the street, on that corner of Thirty-seventh and P. I know one body, the arm went up . . . and I screamed. I never will forget that. I just saw the hand go up. I'd stand out there and watch them burn the bodies and then I'd have nightmares and scream and holler.

The CRC had other divisions besides the burial group. Although other branches of the CRC did not have to handle storm victims' bodies, they still worked hard. The committee in charge of restoring Galveston's water

supply had to contend with the island's broken pumping station, which brought fresh water from mainland Texas before the storm. The hospital committee secured medical care for the injured. The safety committee prevented further harm to life and property by enforcing martial law. The correspondence committee of the CRC had perhaps the most important job of all in the long run: to make public appeals for aid to the world at large.

Until Galveston's links to the outside world were reestablished, however, appeals for help would be pointless. Mail service resumed by boat on September 12. Western Union rewired a single telegraph line on September 13, putting the ruined city back in touch with the outside world. All three of Galveston's railroad

Outside help for Galveston depended on the re-establishment of telegraph communications to the mainland. On September 13, a single telegraph line was reconnected and word of the Galveston tragedy reached Western Union's central office.

bridges (There was an additional bridge to the mainland for wagons.) were passable again just two weeks after the hurricane. Women and children were permitted to leave the island first. The men of Galveston stayed behind for the daunting work of recovery—under a new form of government. The mayor not only deputized members of the citizenry and closed saloons to keep order; he also put the commission form of government into effect after the hurricane. Galveston had 12 city wards; each of these was assigned one "commissary," or relief station. These commissaries collected donations and distributed them to the storm survivors living within their respective wards. Families who lost their breadwinner in the storm got groceries and supplies for free. All able-bodied men who worked in their wards got their relief supplies for free initially. This changed once the city commissions were able to pay the men for their cleanup work. Then, the city expected the workers to buy their own groceries.

Labor unions joined the effort to reclaim the city from the death and the rubble that covered it. The Screwmen's Benevolent Association (Screwmen were skilled dockworkers who packed bales of cotton as tightly as possible into ships using jackscrews.) and its black counterpart, the Cotton Jammers' Association, cleared paths through the rubble, recovered bodies, and sprinkled lime on the ground to promote sanitation. Both the black and the white unions worked mightily to help restore order to the chaotic city, yet black survivors got scant credit. They also received second-rate relief supplies from the commissaries after whites had gotten the better items. Black women who reported to the city commissaries for food and supplies often faced accusations of fraud. White commissary workers suspected them of visiting relief stations outside of their wards to collect extra goods, or of falsely claiming all of their family bread-winners had perished in the storm.

Although Galveston's black community got less of virtually everything the commissaries stocked and experienced more hassles, the commissaries themselves were in no danger of running out of anything. Donations came pouring in soon as mail and shipping services resumed. Disinfectants, potable water, and clothing came in droves to Galveston. So did cash and medical volunteers. So great was the response that Galveston's 12 CRC commissaries could not manage the flow of donations without outside help.

That outside help came in the form of the American National Red Cross. Clara Barton, the organization's 78-year-old founder and president, set off for Galveston on September 13 accompanied by a small group of men and women that included her nephew, Stephen Barton. Miss Barton and the American National Red Cross would focus the nation's attention on making Galveston habitable again.

Relief and Renewal

Clara Barton and her party traveled from Atlanta to New Orleans and finally to Houston, arriving on Galveston Island by boat on September 17. The American National Red Cross was 19 years old when the Galveston Hurricane struck. Even Barton, who had served at the scene of many natural disasters in her long career, was dumbstruck by the devastation at Galveston. She also noticed the haunting emotional numbness of the survivors—even those who had lost their whole families. Clara Barton knew her work was cut out for her. The weather was unseasonably warm now, but before long, autumn would set in, and the homeless would need new shelters. Everyone would need warm clothing. Her managerial skills were needed now, when many people could barely envision having a future in Galveston, more than ever.

Before the 78-year-old Barton could get to work, however, illness forced her to bed for several days. She was determined to spearhead the relief effort in Galveston despite this setback. Her nephew Stephen served as her legs until she regained her strength; he carried out the directives she issued from her bed. The journey to Galveston would be the fiery Clara Barton's final on-site relief mission before her death in 1912. Barton's advancing age did not dampen her enthusiasm for the formidable task of helping the people of Galveston back onto their feet, however.

The American National Red Cross had perfected the art of coming into a disaster area without usurping the authority of local governments. Instead of pushing Mayor Jones and the CRC aside, Clara Barton's organization folded itself into Galveston's leadership and helped it accomplish its goals more efficiently than it could have without help.

Prominent Galveston resident John Sealy donated a four-story warehouse located at 25th and the Strand to the American National Red Cross. Clara Barton contributed her internationally known name to the effort and attracted an even bigger windfall of donations from around the world. The Sealy warehouse became the American National Red Cross headquarters in the city. Each of Galveston's 12 wards had one smaller relief station, in keeping with the model set up by the CRC. Clara Barton assigned members of the CRC specific responsibilities and then interfered as little as possible with their work. In turn, Clara and Stephen Barton were named honorary CRC members.

Soon after Clara Barton and the Red Cross got access to John Sealy's warehouse on the Strand, they transformed it into their busy, active nerve center. The headquarters featured a kitchen to feed those left indigent by the storm, a storage area for donated goods and food, and an orphanage staffed with a teacher. From September 20 to October 31, 1900, the Red Cross headquarters was open from 6:00 A.M. until 10:00 P.M. every day to help those in need.

But some people who approached Clara Barton craved productive work to save their sanity even more than they hungered for donated food. Many women who had survived the hurricane volunteered to help at the headquarters. They overcame their feelings of helplessness and hopelessness by working to aid other storm victims. This surge of hometown volunteerism prompted Barton to found the Galveston Red Cross Auxiliary #1. As we will see later in this chapter, political activism among Galveston women reached new heights in the years after the storm. It is very likely that Clara Barton's example inspired them to become more active in their community than they had ever dreamed possible previously.

Fortunately for the volunteers who needed to help, there was plenty to do. Clara Barton's name and reputation were the two greatest gifts she could have bestowed upon the people of Galveston. The American National Red Cross name, recognized around the world, prompted people and organizations all over the globe to contribute to the hurricane relief effort. The Red Cross headquarters was inundated with household goods, disinfectants, clothing, and cash. Chicago sent two mobile hospital units. People gave as little as twenty-five cents; organizations wrote checks for hundreds of dollars.

One of the most poignant cash donations came from steelworkers in Johnstown, Pennsylvania. Johnstown was the site of what had been America's deadliest flood until the Galveston hurricane struck. The Johnstown Flood occurred in 1889, the result of a break in a dam. (See Sidebar Article.) More than 2000 people drowned. Clara Barton and the American National Red Cross had been there in the flood's aftermath to offer aid. Clara Barton

(continued on page 60)

ANOTHER DEADLY DELUGE: THE JOHNSTOWN FLOOD OF 1889

Most of the residents of Johnstown, a city of 30,000 on Pennsylvania's southwestern side, were not members of the exclusive South Fork Fishing and Hunting Club located 14 miles up the little Conemaugh River. They were largely working-class people who produced iron and steel. Johnstown was prosperous, but built in a dangerous location: right at the fork of two rivers, the Little Conemaugh and the Stony Creek. Flooding was a routine part of the people's lives.

Like Galvestonians before the 1900 hurricane, Johnstown's citizens got so used to minor flooding that they usually just went on about their business whenever it happened. Like the vulnerable Texas barrier island of Galveston, Johnstown was at special risk of suffering sudden and catastrophic flooding. It was not hurricanes that imperiled Johnstown, however. The South Fork Fishing and Hunting Club included Lake Conemaugh, a three-mile-long man-made lake stocked with fish. Only the poorly maintained South Fork Dam prevented Lake Conemaugh from crashing down into Johnstown. Although the city's residents were aware of the threat the dam posed, they carried on with their lives in the valley, their uneasiness returning with each spring's fresh rains.

Friday, May 31, 1889, was raw and wet. Willis Fletcher Johnson, author of the 1889 *History of the Johnstown Flood*, wrote, "It was a dark and stormy day, and amid the darkness and the storm the angel of death spread his wings over the fated valley, unseen, unknown." At 4:07 P.M., the old South Fork Dam finally broke, unleashing 20 million tons of water that hurtled down on Johnstown at 40 miles per hour with a thunderous rumbling.

Ten swift minutes of death and destruction soon followed. People were swept up in a rushing wall of water some 40 feet deep and half a mile wide. Those who didn't drown were either crushed or saved by the huge collection of floating debris that the flood had gathered. An enormous mound of debris piled up against the arches of the Stone Bridge, where Johnstown's two rivers met. When the pile of debris pushing against the bridge caught fire, many victims who had escaped death up to that point perished.

When it was over, 2,209 lives were lost. Until the Galveston Hurricane,

As word of the Galveston disaster spread, aid poured in from around the nation. A very special cash donation came from the residents of Johnstown, Pennsylvania, who had suffered a similarly devastating flood in 1889 in which 2,000 people died.

the Johnstown flood was the deadliest natural disaster in the United States. Survivors blamed members of the South Fork Fishing and Hunting Club for neglecting the dam, but they were not legally liable because the flood was considered an act of God.

As she would do in Galveston over a decade later, Clara Barton brought the American National Red Cross and much-needed relief to Johnstown. Steel baron Andrew Carnegie, who had been a member of the South Fork Fishing and Hunting Club, financed the construction of the Johnstown Flood Museum in 1891. The museum is still open to visitors today.

(continued from page 57)

and her corps of volunteers in Galveston wrote letters of thanks to donors large and small. By the time Barton left Galveston, her image and the Red Cross name had drawn over 17 thousand dollars in cash to the relief effort, and many times that value in material donations.

The Red Cross orphanage located in the upper level of the warehouse had sheltered nearly two-dozen children right after the storm. By the end of October, all of them were reunited with relatives or placed with new adoptive families. As Clara Barton prepared to pull up stakes and leave Galveston, she saw several pressing problems that remained unsolved, however. Fall had come and still many citizens were living in tents. The "white city on the beach" was a community of about 200 Army-issue tents. Others who had lost their homes were squatting in buildings damaged by the storm. Barton started a letter-writing campaign to urge potential donors to provide building materials and labor to rebuild homes lost to the hurricane.

Poor sanitation was an ongoing problem in Galveston. Rubble from destroyed structures was still piled high in many places. Badly decomposed bodies and animal carcasses remained hidden in wreckage, threatening to contaminate the water supply. Galveston officials consulted Dr. George Soper, a sanitation expert from New York City. He urged citizens to be extra vigilant about cleaning animal stalls and stables to help keep the water supply clean, among other recommendations. Dr. Soper was also named an honorary CRC member.

Galveston's electric trolleys were back up before all of the bodies had been cleared from the city. People tried to resume their normal activities against a backdrop of death and destruction. Some enterprising people even saw opportunity in the disaster. "I want to get a cow as soon as I can for there is a great demand for milk

here at good prices, for nearly the whole of the livestock was drowned," wrote dairyman James Brown to
relatives back home in England less than a month
after the storm.

The hurricane had struck just days before a new
school year was to begin in Galveston. Parents were
probably relieved to get their surviving children back into
the rhythm of normal life on October 22, when five
Galveston schools reopened. The reopened schools
comprised four segregated white schools and only one
school for black students. Under the city commission
form of government, blacks had no representation in
Galveston politics. As a result, their schools got the
smallest portion of funding for reconstruction. Galveston's
new city commission form of government (12 mayoral
appointees, all white males, and all responsible for a specific
aspect of city management) left black citizens excluded
from city government. The brave deeds of men like Daniel
Ransom were quickly forgotten after the storm.

Galveston's black community would find itself on the
receiving end of far less relief than white storm survivors
got. The white perception of black Galvestonians as
looters who were failing to pull their weight in the recovery
effort was shaped by gossip and by sensational journalism.
Clara Barton worked with John Gibson, the respected
principle of Galveston's all-black Central High School, to
form a black Red Cross Auxiliary, known as the African
American Red Cross. Even the American National Red
Cross practiced racial prejudice, however. Black hurricane survivors had restricted access to relief stations. They
could only come at certain hours, and then only to receive
whatever goods were left after white storm survivors had
gotten the choicest donations.

Another group traditionally deprived of the right to
vote saw its political power soar in the aftermath of the

storm. White women were the wives, sisters, and daughters of Galveston's white male electorate. Their ability to influence the men who held office—combined with their newfound strength as volunteers in the storm recovery efforts—made them a force to be reckoned with. "Ironically," write Patricia Bellis Bixel and Elizabeth Hayes Turner, "just as black men and women found themselves pleading to be included in official relief circles and the object of unflattering reports, white women became the city's darlings."

On October 31, 1900, the American National Red Cross closed down operations at the borrowed warehouse in Galveston. Although she concentrated her relief efforts on Galveston, Clara Barton also gave areas of mainland Texas affected by the hurricane a much-needed boost: strawberries. Many mainland farmers relied on fruit orchards for their cash crops. Pears, peaches, apples, and plums were abundant before the storm. Afterward, however, leafless, denuded sticks stood where lush, fruited trees had been. Winter was closing in. The farmers needed a new crop that they could raise quickly if they hoped to recover. Strawberries were almost nonexistent on Texas farms, but Clara Barton thought that they held they key to economic survival. She arranged for the shipment of strawberry plants to down-and-out fruit farmers. Her plan worked. To this day, strawberries flourish in Texas.

Introducing strawberries to Texas farmers was one more triumph for Clara Barton's relief effort. Even so, she did receive criticism for using some relief donations to pay her staff. In addition to helping the people of Galveston to regain their financial and emotional footing after an unspeakable disaster, she energized the local women to work for the city's welfare. A group of white women founded the Womens' Health Protective Association (WHPA) before 1901 came to a close. Any

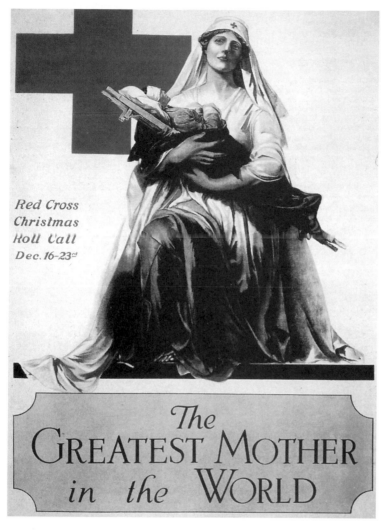

Red Cross
Christmas
Roll Call
Dec. 16-23ʳᵈ

The GREATEST MOTHER in the WORLD

This poignant Red Cross poster from 1918 shows the organization's commitment to rallying aid for victims of disaster or war. Posters like this encourage citizens to donate their time, money, and supplies to relief efforts.

adult white woman in Galveston could join the WHPA. As its name implies, the WHPA dealt with matters of sanitation and public health.

At the time of the Galveston Hurricane, the sanitation practices of dairies, bakeries, restaurants, schools, and jails were not regulated and often inadequate. Dirt was typically visible at the bottom of glass milk bottles, for example. There were no public health laws to prevent bad milk from being sold. Children sometimes died from bacterial infections after drinking bottled milk. People ate at restaurants without ever suspecting that the kitchen might be swarming with flies and filled with garbage.

The women of the WHPA —like all women in Texas at the turn of the century—did not have the right to vote. How did they plan to get public health laws enacted in Galveston? Their volunteer efforts after the hurricane had proven to them and to local officials that women could accomplish a great deal if they worked together. So work together they did, pressuring male friends and relatives who could vote to effect the changes they wanted. The WHPA did their legwork, too. The women broke new ground as they conducted drop-in inspections of restaurants, dairies, prisons, schools—anywhere food was prepared or where their children spent time. When the facilities did not pass muster, the women lobbied male city officials to enact reforms. Most members of the WHPA came from Galveston's upper social classes. They did not discriminate between rich and poor restaurant and shop owners during their sanitation checks, though.

Although the WHPA's members could not work directly for public health reforms because they couldn't vote, they still succeeded in getting laws enacted for cleaner food, water, and lodgings in public places. The group concerned itself with problems directly related to the Galveston hurricane when it first formed. The WHPA initially tackled such issues as disposal of the dead who were still turning up on the island. As time passed and the city's *infrastructure* was rebuilt, the WHPA concentrated on "reflourishing" Galveston. This meant that they took charge of replacing shrubs, trees, and flowers all over the island that were lost in the storm. The women ran a nursery that raised roses, oleanders, and other plants that had been commonplace before the hurricane. Reflourishing did more than just restore the former beauty of neighborhoods hit by the hurricane: it also prevented the soil from eroding. The WHPA funded its activities with a big annual horse show—a tradition that continued until 1910, when automobiles had largely replaced horses. Many members of the WHPA joined the Galveston Equal Suffrage Association (GESA) when that organization was founded in 1912. The efforts of GESA and numerous women's' rights groups around the country chipped away at voting restrictions against women until the Nineteenth Amendment to the United States Constitution guaranteed women's suffrage in 1920.

Life after the Galveston Hurricane slowly returned to some semblance of what it had been before the storm. It would never be the same, however. Survivors were still discovering the skeletons of victims as late as 1908, silent reminders of the water that temporarily swallowed the island city one Saturday in September eight years earlier.

Some of the changes enacted during Galveston's darkest days became permanent. One of them was the commission form of government that had been hastily set up by Mayor Walter C. Jones right after the storm. On July 7, 1901, a new city charter was passed over the protests of sitting city council members. The new Galveston would consist of five commissioners—three of whom would be appointed by Texas governor Joseph Sayers. On September 18, 1901, the new Galveston City Commission took office. Judge William T. Austin was elected the city's new mayor-president. Police and fire commissioner A.P. Norman was also elected to office. The governor tapped the other three: I.H. Kempner was appointed commissioner of finance and revenue; Valery Austin was named commissioner of streets and public improvements, and Herman C. Lange became the head of water and sewer in Galveston.

The commission government system needed a little refining, however. Galveston voters wanted a more democratic election process; so all five commissioners were eventually elected officials rather than appointees. More than 70 U.S. cities would be running commission governments modeled after Galveston's by 1910. The commission form of government lasted in Galveston until 1960.

Once life in Galveston had returned to some semblance of normal, the need to prevent another storm like the hurricane of 1900 from destroying the city again was undeniable. If Galveston wished to avoid the fate of the abandoned port city of Indianola, the City Commission would have to take immediate action.

It was apparent to just about everyone that a protective seawall would need to be built around Galveston. Still, the City Commission was wary of taking that step. They were afraid that the rest of the world would see constructing a seawall as an admission that Galveston was in immediate danger of a repeat of the 1900 hurricane. This might scare vacationers away from Galveston's warm Gulf beaches and deter investors from developing businesses in the city. Who would visit or build in Galveston if everything was in danger of being smashed to bits a second time?

Galveston could not afford to discourage business or tourism because the city had already been on shaky financial ground before the storm. After the devastating hurricane and cleanup, the beautiful island paradise was in a staggering amount of debt. Despite the city's modern conveniences and confident, vibrant citizenry, Houston had already begun to overshadow Galveston as Texas's premier city before the hurricane completed the eclipse.

On November 20, 1901, the City Commission selected

a board of engineers to design and build a seawall around Galveston. Construction finally started on October 27, 1902. The wall measures 17 feet high, has a varying width of at least 16 feet at the bottom and three to five feet at the top. The wall is made mostly of concrete with wooden pilings. The first installment was finished in 1904: it protected 3.3 miles of beach on the Gulf side of Galveston. A second segment that shielded the military installation at Fort Crockett ran from 39th to 53rd and was completed in 1905. The final addition to the seawall was finished in 1962. The Galveston seawall protects a third of the city's Gulf coastline today. The entire cost to the city—in financial

To ensure there would be no repeat of the Galveston disaster, the city began construction of a massive concrete seawall in 1901. With the final section completed in 1962, the wall protects Galveston's coastline from storm surges.

crisis at the time of the earliest construction—was more than 14 million dollars.

The expense of the seawall would have been wasted, however, if Galveston did not also do something to raise the elevation of the city and its structures. The grade-raising project was begun in late 1903 and completed by 1910. It consisted of jacking up buildings (including houses), fire hydrants, streets—the entire infrastructure of the city—and filling the space beneath with sand dredged from the Gulf. Extremely large buildings like the Ursuline Convent were impossible to lift, so they had their bottom floors filled in with sand.

The grade raising necessitated a canal that ran parallel to the seawall to transport the fill to different areas in the city. Houses were moved to clear a path for the canal, creating new neighborhoods in some cases. Unfortunately, not everyone was pleased with this development. Many residents were also upset because they had to pay for the raising of their homes and business out of their own pockets. Property owners directly in the canal's planned path did not have to pay to have their homes and businesses moved, though. They did not have to pay property taxes during the grade raising, either—a development that angered some who were not right in the canal's path, but were forced to move their houses at their own expense.

Others took advantage of the grade raising to enjoy picnic lunches along the canal or to dump unwanted household goods under their homes for burial in the fill. Galvestonians also adjusted to getting around the city on wooden catwalks during the grade-raising years. When the fill started pumping in under their houses, people sometimes had the family chickens or goats temporarily living in their kitchens! Many people learned to enjoy some aspects of the project despite the inconveniences it caused.

Galveston's grade-raising project increased the city on a sandbar's elevation to 17 feet right behind the seawall to a low of 10 feet on Broadway. After the grade-raising project, many people felt confident that Galveston, with its new seawall, could reasonably expect to survive a natural disaster like the 1900 hurricane reasonably well.

A hurricane in 1909 made some minor repairs to the seawall necessary, but its first true test came during the predawn hours of August 17, 1915. A hurricane of similar force made landfall at approximately the same place as the 1900 hurricane had. Winds howled at up to 120 miles per hour and waves over 20 feet high battered the seawall. Morning came with just eight deaths reported in Galveston. The seawall and grade raising had done their job. This added safety came at a price, however. Even today, sand from the Gulf is dredged up and placed on Galveston's beaches to help combat the constant erosion of the shoreline caused by the seawall.

As we can see, the Galveston Hurricane continues to have repercussions on the city even today.

Although St. Patrick's Church was heavily damaged by the 1900 hurricane, the structure was repaired and lifted on jacks to replace silt with a new elevated foundation. The church is the heaviest of the island's structures successfully raised in this way.

Galveston Reborn

6

The sandbar metropolis of Galveston was emerging from ruin. Life was returning to normal—but clearly a new kind of normal. All told, the 1900 hurricane had cut short some 6,000 lives on the island and as many as 4,000 more on the Texas mainland. Skeletons turned up on the island periodically as late as 1908. Families who had no bodies to bury after the hurricane hung memorial certificates on their walls for lost loved ones and painted high-water marks on homes left standing after the storm tide receded.

Although most survivors did not go into great detail when they recounted the long-ago night of horror for their children and grandchildren, the hurricane permanently wove itself into the fabric of life in Galveston. Historians taped interviews with survivors decades after the storm. The experience of living through it affected the social customs of later generations. Author Gary Cartwright noted that even today, "A bride is expected to send wedding invitations to total strangers if *her* grandparents spent the night with *their* grandparents during the 1900 storm."

Progress marched on. Galveston's harbor had space for 500 ships. The first loads of cotton after the 1900 hurricane left the port of Galveston in October of that year. The storm had swept all 14 of Galveston's black churches out to sea; but by 1910, 15 new ones had been built. In 1912, a causeway two miles long linked Galveston to mainland Texas. It featured two train tracks, an electric train track, and car lanes. A drawbridge at the center of the causeway allowed boat traffic through Galveston Bay.

For all of the good news about Galveston after the hurricane, however, there were some signs that the disaster had spelled the end of the city's heyday. There was an immigration station right in Galveston Harbor on tiny Pelican Island. Galveston was the first American city that new immigrants would set foot upon, but employers and ordinary citizens alike gave them a cool reception. The people of Galveston failed to embrace the incoming—and often highly motivated—workers, prompting many immigrants to settle elsewhere. This loss of willing workers prevented businesses from growing as much as they could have, and it meant that there were fewer people available to pay for goods and services in Galveston. To the northeast, Houston was poised to take Galveston's place as the most important harbor in Texas. The mainland city had its ship channel dug deeper in 1914. Houston soon became not only a premier commercial port city, but it also welcomed military ships, whose crews would re-supply themselves in the city, further spurring the economy there.

The discovery of oil in Houston decisively ended Galveston's bid to be the most developed and progressive city in Texas. Once, proud islanders made snide comments about stingy day-trippers from Houston coming to Galveston's beaches. Now, however, even their meager tourist dollars would have been welcome. The crown of the "Queen City of the Gulf" had become tarnished after the 1900 hurricane. The up-and-coming Texas cities of Dallas and San Antonio also stole some of Galveston's former glory during the early 20th century.

A decline in prominence may have ruptured Galveston's old sense of pride, but the city's people persevered. The Port of Galveston remained the city's main source of income. But there were less than legitimate businesses in the city, too. Until law enforcement locked down on the gambling and prostitution industries in the early 1950s, Galveston had a slightly exotic image because of it offered visitors both nighttime vices and warm beach days. Pleasure seekers called the city the Free State of Galveston.

One bit of Galveston lore stars Jim Simpson, an attorney who left the island for Texas City in part because he was frustrated by Galveston's lawlessness. He joined forces with Texas attorney general Will Wilson to take back the city from the Maceo crime family, who operated the biggest illegal gambling racket on the island. After Simpson confiscated a huge stash of slot machines and other games of chance, he disposed of them by loading them onto a barge and dumping them into the sea. This bit of showmanship hit a snag when Simpson discovered that slot machines float!

Even though big-time illegal gambling came to an end in a scene better suited to a comedy than to a Hollywood crime drama, Simpson and Attorney General

Wilson got the job done. The Maceo family lost its hold over Galveston. In more recent years, proposals to introduce legal, casino-style gambling to Galveston have been voted down more than once.

Legitimate businesses carried on in Galveston, too. There was also an air force base on the island during World War II that was the last stop for pilots headed to combat over the Pacific. The Medical Branch of the University of Texas employs many Galvestonians to this day. Other important industries include commercial fishing and, of course, tourism. In 1900, Galveston boasted a population of approximately 38 thousand; today, that number exceeds 60 thousand. Although some say that the island has grown and developed as much as it can, native-born islanders tend to stay put and maintain a stubborn pride in Galveston.

Isaac Monroe Cline—originally from Tennessee— did not have deep roots in Galveston's sand. After the storm, his children were motherless, but he remained single for the rest of his life. He also left Galveston for New Orleans. Cline became so serious about his hobbies, painting and art collecting, that he sold art in New Orleans after being forced to retire from the weather service in 1935. He was already over 70 years old.

Isaac Monroe Cline died in 1955, never having forgotten the deadly hurricane of 1900 or his role in it. He changed the focus of his studies from the weather's effects on health to the behavior of hurricanes. Isaac Cline successfully showed that a hurricane's greatest threat to human life came in the form of wind-driven storm tides, not the winds themselves.

"But a question haunted him: Did some of the blame for all those deaths in Galveston belong to him?" writes Erik Larson in *Isaac's Storm*. Cline's wife Cora died because the family stayed in their house. Dr. Cline and his younger brother Joseph eventually stopped speaking altogether in the years after the storm. They went to their respective graves without ever settling their differences. As Joseph's superior at the weather station, Isaac had disregarded Joseph's urging to call for the evacuation of Galveston when there was still enough time to save lives. "Maybe each time Isaac saw Joseph," Larson suggests, "the magnitude of his own error came roaring back to him."

Had the Clines been tracking the Galveston Hurricane today, perhaps the terrible death toll on the island—and the brothers' subsequent rift—could have been avoided. Weather satellites now orbit the earth, transmitting images that help meteorologists spot the formation of tropical depressions and predict with some accuracy the path they will take if they become hurricanes.

Data from satellites has helped scientists determine that approximately five hurricanes strike coastal areas in the United States during every three-year period. Of these five hurricanes, two will probably pose a significant threat to life and property: these two storms will measure a Category 3 or greater on the Saffir-Simpson Scale (see sidebar).

Even before satellites could help track hurricanes, however, a few intrepid airplane pilots began flying into storms to get information about their wind speed, direction, air pressure, and other measurements. These Hurricane Hunters began flying their first missions in 1944; today the Hurricane Hunters are Air Force reservists who fly out of Keesler Air Force Base in Mississippi and MacDill Air Force Base in Florida. They record data for the National Oceanic and Atmospheric Administration's (NOAA) National Hurricane Center, located in Miami, Florida. Information gathered by Hurricane Hunter jets for NOAA has no doubt

(continued on page 78)

THE SAFFIR-SIMPSON SCALE

In 1969, an engineer named Herbert Saffir collaborated with Dr. Bob Simpson, then the director of the National Hurricane Center, to develop a system that rated a hurricane's destructive capacity due to wind damage and flooding. The Saffir-Simpson Scale uses a hurricane's wind speed as its main variable. This is because wind speed determines in large part how high storm surges will be. The scale is sometimes also called the Saffir-Simpson Damage Potential Scale. By either name, it gives weather experts a basis for comparison between hurricanes in terms of instensity. The Saffir-Simpson Scale also helps forecasters project just how dangerous a coming storm will be and to advise the people living in its path appropriately. Public officials use it to help them decide whether or not to order evacuations. The example of the Saffir-Simpson Scale below appears on the website of the Atlantic Oceanographic and Meteorological Laboratory (AOML), a research facility that is part of the National Oceanic and Atmospheric Administration (NOAA). *[www.aoml.noaa.gov]*

A Category One hurricane has wind speeds ranging from 74 to 95 miles per hour. No real damage to building structures. Damage primarily to unanchored mobile homes, shrubbery, and trees. Also, some coastal road flooding and minor pier damage.

A Category Two hurricane has wind speeds ranging from 96 to 110 miles per hour. Some roofing material, door, and window damage to buildings. Considerable damage to vegetation, mobile homes, and piers. Coastal and low-lying escape routes flood two to four hours before arrival of center. Small craft in unprotected anchorages break moorings.

A Category Three hurricane has wind speeds ranging from 111 to 130 miles per hour. Some structural damage to small residences and utility buildings with a minor amount of curtainwall [exterior walls of buildings that don't bear weight] failures. Mobile homes are destroyed. Flooding near the coast destroys smaller structures with larger structures damaged by floating debris. Terrain continuously lower than five feet above sea level may be flooded inland eight miles or more.

A Category Four hurricane has wind speeds ranging from 131 to 155 miles per hour. More extensive curtainwall failures with some complete roof structure failure on small residences. Major erosion of beach. Major damage to lower

Storm prediction technology has come a long way since the Galveston disaster. Since the 1940s, storm trackers called "Hurricane Hunters" have used sophisticated instruments and special airplanes to fly through storms and gather valuable information on barometric pressure, wind speed, rotation, rainfall, and storm track.

floors of structures near the shore. Terrain continuously lower than 10 feet above sea level may be flooded, requiring massive evacuation of residential areas inland as far as six miles. The Galveston Hurricane of 1900 is thought to have been a Category Four storm.

A Category Five hurricane has wind speeds in excess of 155 miles per hour. Complete roof failure on many residences and industrial buildings. Some complete building failures with small utility buildings blown over or away. Major damage to lower floors of all structures located less than 15 feet above sea level and within 500 yards of the shoreline. Massive evacuation of residential areas on low ground within five to ten miles of the shoreline may be required.

(continued from page 75)

saved many lives by catching potentially deadly hurricanes early enough to evacuate populous coastal areas.

On a typical 10 to 11-hour flight into a hurricane, the six-person crew consists of a commander, a co-pilot, a flight engineer, a navigator, a weather officer, and a dropsonde operator. A Hurricane Hunter plane starts surveying the hurricane at altitudes of just 500 to 1500 feet, but reaches heights of up to 45,000 feet as it passes in and out of the storm. Pilots even fly into the treacherous eye wall, where winds are fastest and rainfall is the heaviest. The dropsonde is an expendable instrument on a parachute. The dropsonde operator releases it from the plane. As it drifts down and then lands on the ocean's surface, the dropsonde sends radio signals indicating the air pressure, wind speed and direction, temperature, and humidity inside the hurricane. Thanks to the Hurricane Hunters, scientists can construct good theoretical models that help them accurately predict the height of the storm tides an approaching hurricane will produce, for instance.

The Air Force also employs the Hurricane Hunters for many other tasks, such as studying oil spills on the ocean. They can even do aerial counts of marine mammal populations.

Hurricane Carla

In 1961, Galveston had the benefits of better prediction techniques when Hurricane Carla started heading for the island. It was Thursday, September 8—the sixty-first anniversary of the deadliest storm the United States had ever known. The following Sunday night found evacuees actually coming *into* Galveston from parts of the Texas mainland. This was because of the seawall; it was preferable to wait out the hurricane on a sandbar island with a seawall than in some places on the unprotected mainland coast. On the afternoon of Monday, September 12, Carla veered southwest of Galveston. Before islanders could breathe a sigh of relief, however, two tornadoes triggered by Carla hit Galveston the next day, killing seven, destroying buildings, and knocking power and water out of many neighborhoods for days.

Although Carla snatched relatively few lives from Galveston and spared the island from the worst of her destruction, people were still shaken. The seawall may have helped control flooding, but Galvestonians realized that they were still at the mercy of the winds—or even tornadoes—that hurricanes can spawn. The sprawling Ursuline Convent—where one thousand people found safe shelter and four babies were born during the 1900 hurricane—sustained severe tornado damage. Yet, instead of scrambling to rebuild it, Galveston's Catholic leaders let the convent and its adjoining school sit in disrepair. The school was knocked down soon after the storm. The Ursuline Convent had stood in Galveston since 1847. After Hurricane Carla's near miss, it was a frail shell of the sturdy, lifesaving structure it once was. It finally met the same end as the school in the early 1970s.

What happened to the descendants of the 1900 hurricane's survivors? Where was the defiant spirit of their ancestors, who had chosen to rebuild Galveston and raise families on the island despite the risks? Historian Gary Cartwright believes that Hurricane Carla's tornadoes left Galvestonians too shaken and frazzled to remain optimistic in the wake of nature's fury:

> Most people planned to stay, of course, but there was a palpable change in attitude, a loss of nerve, a rupture of values. Suddenly, people seemed tired of the past, tired of being reminded of their history and legacy.

Whatever the causes, Cartwright says that for years after Carla brushed by Galveston, the city went into decline. People didn't seem to care about restoring or preserving Galveston's beautiful Victorian architecture. The Strand, once the hub of the city, had become a hang-out for the homeless.

The Ursuline Convent had been wrecked over the protests of a few people who were interested in preserving grand old Galveston. These people—many of them not native to the city—became more vocal and more visible, raising money to restore they Queen City of the Gulf's past glory. Their efforts helped Galveston survive the turbulent 1970s. Although she missed Galveston, Hurricane Carla briefly revealed the residue of fear and despair that still hung over the city generations after the hurricane of 1900.

A brief overview of three hurricanes the struck the United States during the twentieth century follows. Clearly, hurricanes can end lives and destroy people's dreams along with their homes and businesses, just as the Galveston Hurricane once did. But emerging storm detection and weather prediction technologies have given humankind an edge in the battle to save lives since that fateful Saturday in September of 1900.

Hurricane Camille

Hurricane Camille smashed into the Mississippi coast on the night of August 17, 1969. Camille was a Category Five storm. The only twentieth century hurricane stronger than Camille devastated the Florida Keys on September 2, 1935. This storm hit before the Tropical Prediction Center started assigning names to hurricanes (see sidebar): therefore, it is commonly known as the Florida Keys Labor Day Storm. Camille had passed through Cuba on her way to the states, killing three.

Scientists could only guess at Camille's wind speeds because they were so very high. Many believe that she

packed gusts of about 200 miles per hour. The hurricane pushed storm tides over 24 feet high onto the Mississippi coast. Camille's furious waters claimed 143 lives from coastal Alabama to Louisiana. The death toll could have been much worse, however, had it not been for the use of an airplane to help predict Camille's path and behavior. A flight into the storm early on August 17 led experts to believe that the hurricane's storm surge would be much, much higher than the 12 feet they had originally predicted. Additional last-minute evacuations of coastal areas based on data from that flight probably saved numerous lives.

In 1969, Hurricane Camille again tested the Gulf Coast's storm defenses. Emergency evacuations of coastal residents based on weather predictions saved countless lives from the storm's rampage.

WHY WE NAME HURRICANES

The Galveston Hurricane of 1900 took thousands of lives long before the National Weather Service officially began the practice of giving hurricanes personal names in 1953. When Galvestonians today speak of "the storm," however, it still goes without saying that they are talking about the 1900 hurricane.

Why, then, is it a good idea to give hurricanes individual names? Simplicity is the main reason: before hurricanes had names, meteorologists referred to them by their longitude and latitude. This was both long-winded and confusing, since storm systems are constantly on the move and their coordinates change constantly. Furthermore, storm systems can last for weeks before they dissipate. This means that multiple tropical depressions, tropical storms, and hurricanes might be in various stages of development in a given area at one time. Giving each storm its own name prevents confusion when meteorologists are tracking more than one hurricane. It also helps emergency personnel and the general public to know exactly which storm(s) they need to watch closely.

The idea of giving hurricanes personal names is not new. A nineteenth-century meteorologist in Australia reportedly named the tropical storms he tracked after women. During World War II, meteorologists in the U.S. military tracked tropical cyclones over the Pacific Ocean. To keep tabs on individual storm systems, they gave each one a feminine personal name (often naming storms after their wives or female relatives). In 1953, the National Weather Service adopted the practice of giving hurricanes women's names. In the spirit of equal opportunity, the National Weather Service was also using men's names for cyclones over both the Atlantic and the Pacific by 1979.

Other places in the world use different systems to name their tropical cyclones. Cyclones in the North Indian Ocean aren't assigned names at all. A sample list of the National Weather Service's Atlantic, Gulf of Mexico, and Caribbean Sea hurricane names for the 2003 storm season appears below. Notice that women's and men's names now alternate.

2003: Ana, Bill, Claudette, Danny, Erika, Fabian, Grace, Henri, Isabel, Juan, Kate, Larry, Mindy, Nicholas, Odette, Peter, Rose, Sam, Theresa, Victor, Wanda.

After an especially lethal or destructive hurricane, the National Weather Service retires its name so it will never be used again. The list of retired hurricane names includes Carla (1961), Camille (1969), and Andrew (1992).

HURRICANE ANDREW
24 AUG 1992

After her initial rampage, Camille tracked northeast to West Virginia and southern Virginia. She ran out of steam, weakening to a tropical depression. Nevertheless, Camille was far from harmless. She dumped up to 25 inches of rain in some areas, causing 113 more deaths. The total price of Hurricane Camille's destructive journey exceeded $1.4 billion.

Hurricane Andrew

The most expensive natural disaster in U.S. history, Hurricane Andrew left behind approximately $25 billion in losses in August of 1992. But Andrew's staggering price tag doesn't begin to tell the story of the human suffering he left in his wake. The storm killed some 65 people, but left as many as a quarter million more homeless. South Florida bore the brunt of Andrew's assault; the southern part of Louisiana and the Bahamas were also affected, however.

Satellite technology has allowed us to gain valuable early-warning data on hurricanes from high above the storms. This image of Hurricane Andrew in 1992 shows the storm's transatlantic course as it approached the U.S. coast.

Andrew was a small hurricane that packed a powerful punch at Category Four. Wind speeds raged at up to 175 miles per hour. He made landfall in Florida in the early morning hours of August 24th. Dade County, Florida, experienced storm tides measuring over 15 feet. Hurricane warnings and evacuation of southeastern Florida's coastline and south central Louisiana probably prevented the death toll from being much higher than it was.

Hurricane Opal

Hurricane Opal was another storm that concentrated her fury on Florida, making landfall on as a Category Three storm on October 4, 1995. Unlike Andrew, however, Opal's target of choice was the Florida panhandle, near Pensacola. Opal also affected parts of Alabama, Georgia, and Mississippi. She left behind some $3 billion in losses in America and killed people in Guatemala and Mexico as well as in the United States during her erratic life cycle.

Opal originated on September 11th off Africa's west coast. She did not make the leap from tropical depression to tropical storm until September 30th off Mexico's Yucatan Peninsula. She then wheeled into the Gulf of Mexico and tracked towards Florida. Opal quickly made up for lost time, unexpectedly strengthening to a Category Four hurricane during the early morning hours of October 4th. One reason for Opal's rapid, ferocious transformation was the Gulf of Mexico's extremely warm temperature. At approximately 83°F, the warm ocean fed Opal mist and helped her intensify quickly.

Hurricane Opal hit Pensacola as a Category Three hurricane and weakened quickly without the warm ocean to fuel her. Still, Pensacola experienced winds from 125 to 150 miles per hour. Most devastating to the to the Florida panhandle's coast was a storm surge of up to 14 feet that caused heavy property damage. Fortunately, the tide did not sweep anybody out to sea with it.

Hurricane Opal proved murderous by other means, though. She unleashed tornadoes in Florida, killing one. She spawned a significant tornado in Maryland, too. Opal caused a total of eight other U.S. deaths in addition to the one in Florida. These other fatalities were all the result of falling trees, and they occurred in Alabama, Georgia, and North Carolina. Opal's death tolls in Guatemala (31) and in Mexico (19) resulted from flooding during her maturation into a hurricane.

Although Hurricane Hunter planes logged a total of about 122 flight hours in their studies of Opal, she was still more intense than anyone had anticipated because of her rapid surge in strength over the Gulf. Sometimes, our post-Galveston technologies are still no match for nature's whims.

A lonely survivor, St. Patrick's Church stands amid the ruins of Galveston. The structure was repaired after the flood and continues to stand today.

An American Hurricane Problem?

In the nineteenth century, European settlers to Galveston Island ridiculed the Karankawa Indians they encountered there for their tendency to cry easily. Little did they know that generations later, all of Galveston would be in tears—tears both openly wept and tears staunchly held back—after the terrible night of September 8, 1900. The Galveston Hurricane changed the people who stayed to rebuild. Family stories abound to this day, although many are sketchy in the details. This suggests that survivors were either too stunned or too saddened to discuss the storm as they grew older. Philip Gordie Tipp, who worked in a dead gang as a young man of 18, later wrote that the Galveston Hurricane left him "never able to sit down" more than 60 years after the fact.

The late summer of 2000 brought renewed interest in the great hurricane and the stories surrounding it. As the centennial of the storm drew near, a story in the *Houston Chronicle* entitled "Tales of Courage: Many Unable to Talk About Disaster" neatly summed up the century of silence. "I ended up with nothing [details about the storm]," remarked one granddaughter of a storm survivor. "I think it was just such a horrendous experience. I think it was like we find with these veterans after they go through these horrible battles."

One survivor did open up to the *Chronicle*'s Kevin Moran about the 1900 hurricane. She was 104-year-old Lorraine Hofeller, who lived through the storm with her mother, father, and older brother at 2012 Broadway, her childhood home. Hofeller recalled sitting on her mother's lap "all night" as a frightened four-year-old. She also acknowledged being extremely afraid of bad weather since having survived the storm.

On September 9, 2000, a 10-foot-tall bronze sculpture by David W. Moore depicting a man, woman, and baby clinging together was dedicated to both the victims and the survivors of the Galveston Hurricane. The sculpture stands at Seawall Boulevard and 48th Street. One person on hand for the dedication was a man named Wes Williams—the grandson of Isaac Monroe Cline.

One might reasonably wonder why anyone who lived through the Galveston Hurricane would have wanted to stay on the island. But most did. Perhaps it is the soothing, tepid Gulf beaches, the lure of life on the water. But Galveston's island paradise comes with a price: the perils of living on a sandbar.

Not only is Galveston a barrier island vulnerable to deadly tropical weather events; its very shape is also constantly changing because of beach erosion. The seawall erected after the hurricane is slowly destroying the beach even as it protects the lives of those who live behind it. "Seawalls work by reflecting the energy of waves; unfortunately, they reflect it back on the beach, which is washed out to sea and carried away by currents," observes Gary Cartwright. In areas unprotected by the seawall, the Gulf of Mexico is inching ever closer to expensive beachfront properties. There is a danger that an intense hurricane could even break the island into two pieces.

Everyone who owns a home in Galveston knows that an intense hurricane will come: it is a question of when, not if. Thanks to advance warning systems and the seawall, another Category Four hurricane with a track similar to the one that struck Galveston in 1900 would probably never again exact such a high death toll.

The news is not all good, though. The only way out of Galveston in the event of another such storm is the causeway linking the island city to the mainland. Galveston runs a ferry to mainland Texas, but this would be shut down for obvious reasons in the event of threatening weather. The causeway would be jammed with cars if an evacuation were called, since Galveston's population now exceeds 60,000. (That figure was under 40,000 in 1900.)

There are no easy answers when it comes to developing fragile barrier islands like Galveston. As more people crave sun-drenched residences—and vacation homes—all along America's coasts, buildings will continue to pop up like seaweed. Unlike more random natural disasters such as earthquakes, hurricanes occur in some parts of the United States with predictable regularity. This means that home and business owners in coastal areas can and should expect repeated storm damage to their properties. When hurricane Georges struck the resort area of Dauphin Island, Alabama, in 1998, homeowners experienced their fifth significant hurricane in 20 years!

Who pays for rebuilding in hurricane-prone coastal

areas like Dauphin Island, Galveston, and countless other seaside communities in America? Private insurers have long been afraid of being wiped out by the cost of issuing policies for beachfront properties that will need repairs again and again. That's where the federal government comes in. The government subsidizes flood insurance for owners of high-risk property. With no reserve to dip into in times of real disaster, the government relies on tax dollars to help pay out damage claims from these repeat storm victims and their repetitive losses. In 1998, two percent of all homes participating in the National Flood Insurance Program comprised a whopping one-third of that year's $8.6 billion in damage claims.

Despite the National Flood Insurance Program's pay-outs to homeowners in hurricane-prone areas, the federal government has no authority to make rules governing where beachfront homes can be built. The decision of whether or not to set homes back a certain distance from the shoreline is made by local governments. The Federal Emergency Management Agency (FEMA), which administers the National Flood Insurance Program's funding, is currently obligated to fund rebuilding of vulnerable houses, but it has no clout to force builders to fortify these houses against future hurricanes. Although some communities do have rules in place to require storm shutters, special windows and other improvements by law, many others don't. People are free to build over and over again in storm-prone areas, yet they are not obligated to take any steps to avoid future hurricane damage.

More worrisome than any amount of money wasted is the potential danger to people who build in storm-prone coastal areas. Hurricane experts say that another big storm is bound to come to the United States. The 1970s and 1980s were periods of relatively low hurricane activity in the United States. This sets people currently living in

As more people build shorefront homes and businesses, more residents risk the wrath of hurricane winds and tidal surges. Here, workmen shore up a Miami cafe in preparation for Hurricane Erin in 1995.

coastal areas up for peril because many of them have never experienced a major hurricane. They may have a false sense of security and fail to take evacuation orders seriously. Even if homeowners did take an order to evacuate seriously, the unprecedented level of traffic congestion along U.S. coastal areas would make getting everyone out of a massive storm's path in time difficult.

According to NOAA, the population boom in coastal areas poses a real threat to life in the future:

> The United States has a significant hurricane problem. Our shorelines attract large numbers of people. From Maine to Texas, our coastline is filled with new homes, condominium towers, and cities built on sand waiting for the next storm to threaten its [sic] residents and their dreams.

For many individuals, the sun, sand, and surf make the risk worthwhile. Since the trend towards building and rebuilding vulnerable coastal properties is not likely to reverse itself as long as people are willing to take their chances for a house on the beach, preparation is the best defense (see hurricane safety sidebar). The story of the Galveston Hurricane shows just how fiercely people will cling to their homes—even if home rests on nothing more than a perilously beautiful sliver of sand.

HURRICANE SAFETY

It is vital to know the difference between a hurricane watch and a hurricane warning as you prepare for a coming storm.

* A hurricane watch is an advisory for a coastal area that a hurricane is possible within the next 36 hours.

* A hurricane warning is an announcement that a storm with sustained winds of 74 miles per hour or faster is coming to a coastal area within the next 24 hours. Winds may be of less than hurricane strength and still warrant a hurricane warning if hazardous coastal flooding and exceptionally high waves occur with the winds.

If you live in a landfalling hurricane's projected path, a little advance planning will make coping with a dangerous storm easier and may even save your life. If you have time, board up your home's windows and put away anything that could become a flying missile in hurricane-force winds. This includes lawn furniture, outdoor toys, bicycles, and swings.

Stay tuned to radio and/or TV broadcasts. If it is recommended that you evacuate your home and move inland, it is imperative that you do so! Many people currently living in America's coastal areas have never experienced a major hurricane (Category Three or higher). This inexperience can lead to a false sense of security. Select your destination beforehand; you may choose a shelter set up specifically for the hurricane in a secure building, or the home of a friend or relative outside of the affected area. If you drive, pack a road map in case flooding forces you to take an unfamiliar alternate route. Don't try to drive over flooded roads!

If you plan to weather the storm at home, make sure to assemble a survival kit well in advance of the hurricane. It should include, at minimum, the following:

- A manual can opener and non-perishable canned foods and juices.

- Water: the American Red Cross recommends storing one gallon per person per day.

- A first aid kit and any prescription medicines you or your family members will need. Also include insect repellant and sunscreen.

- Flashlights (never use candles for light) and a battery-powered radio with a supply of extra batteries.

- Basic bathroom supplies such as toilet paper, soap, and diapers, if needed.

- Raincoats, sturdy boots, work gloves, extra blankets and sleeping bags.

- A small amount of cash, your insurance documents, your driver's license or other form of photo identification.

Stay tuned to your radio and/or TV during the hurricane if possible. The most important things you can do are to remain calm and to stay indoors and away from windows, which can shatter if hit by flying debris. Remain tuned into radio and/or TV after the storm. Avoid going outside or driving—especially if you live near a river or a small stream—until local officials advise that the danger has decreased. Once outdoors, beware of downed power lines as well as storm drains and drainage ditches.

Chronology

1891   Isaac Monroe Cline writes in the *Galveston News* that the island city is in no danger of being devastated by a severe hurricane

1900   *September 8:* A hurricane now believed to have been a Category Four storm makes landfall in Galveston, Texas, killing 6,000 islanders and some 4,000 more people on the Texas mainland

       September 9: Galveston mayor Walter C. Jones declares martial law

       September 11: Approximately 700 bodies buried at sea in Gulf of Mexico return to shore, necessitating mass cremations of the dead

       September 12: Mail service restored to Galveston by boat

       September 13: Single telegraph line restored to island

       September 20-October 31: Clara Barton and American National Red Cross operate a relief station at 25th and the Strand

       October 22: The first schools reopen in Galveston

1901   White Galveston women found Women's Health Protective Association (WHPA)

       September 18: Galveston installs new city commission form of government

1902   *October 27:* Construction begins on Galveston Seawall

1912   Causeway built connecting Galveston Island and mainland Texas; Galveston Equal Suffrage Association (GESA) is founded

1915   *August 17:* Hurricane of comparable severity to 1900 storm hits Galveston, killing eight on the island

1944   First Hurricane Hunter planes used to track storms

1961   *September 13:* Hurricane Carla does not make landfall in Galveston, but tornadoes resulting from Carla kill seven and damage buildings on the island

1969   Herbert Saffir and Dr. Bob Simpson formulate the Saffir-Simpson
       Scale to rate the intensity of hurricanes in terms of their potential
       to cause damage

2000   *September 9:* Bronze sculpture by David W. Moore dedicated to
       victims and survivors of 1900 storm in Galveston

Further Reading

Books and Articles

Bixel, Patricia Bellis and Elizabeth Hayes Turner. *Galveston and the 1900 Storm*. Austin: The University of Texas Press, 2000.

Cartwright, Gary. *Galveston: a History of the Island*. NY: Atheneum, 1991.

Cline, Isaac M. *Storms, Floods and Sunshine*. New Orleans: Pelican Press, 1945

Greene, Casey Edward and Shelly Henley Kelly, eds. *Through a Night of Horrors: Voices from the 1900 Galveston Storm*. College Station, TX: Texas A&M University Press, 2000.

Greene, Nathan C., ed. *Story of the 1900 Galveston Hurricane*. 1900. New edition. Gretna, LA: Pelican Publishing Company, Inc., 2000.

Larson, Erik. *Isaac's Storm*. New York: Vintage Books, 2000.

Moran, Kevin, comp. "Tales of Courage: Many Unable to Talk About Disaster," *Houston Chronicle,* 24 August 2000.

_____ . "104-Year-Old Tells How She Survived 1900 Hurricane," *Houston Chronicle,* 7 September 2000.

Olafson, Steve. "Unimaginable Devastation: Deadly Storm Came with Little Warning," *Houston Chronicle,* 28 August 2000.

Weems, John Edward. *A Weekend in September.* 1957. Reprint. College Station, TX: Texas A&M University Press, 1980.

Web Sites

"Reason to Name Hurricanes"
"The United States Hurricane Problem"
   [http://www.aoml.noaa.gov/general/lib/reason.html]

"Before the Hurricane"
"During the Hurricane"
"After the Hurricane"
   [http://www.usatoday.com/weather/disasters/whurdur.htm]

"Hurricane Hunters"
   [http://www.fema.gov/kids/huhunt.htm]

"Hurricane Awareness: Storm Surge"
   [http.www.nhc.noaa.gov/HAW/day1/storm_surge.htm]

"Johnstown Flood Museum"
   [http: www.paturnpike.com/traveler/fall97/fpage4.htm]

Index

Index

Picture Credits

KRISTINE BRENNAN is a writer and editor in the Philadelphia area, where she lives with her husband and sons. She holds a B.A. in English with a concentration in professional writing from Elizabethtown College. She is also the author of *The Stock Market Crash of 1929* and *The Chernobyl Nuclear Disaster* in this series.

JILL McCAFFREY has served for four years as national chairman of the Armed Forces Emergency Services of the American Red Cross. Ms. McCaffrey also serves on the board of directors for Knollwood—the Army Distaff Hall. The former Jill Ann Faulkner, a Massachusetts native, is the wife of Barry R. McCaffrey, who served in President Bill Clinton's cabinet as director of the White House Office of National Drug Control Policy. The McCaffreys are the parents of three grown children: Sean, a major in the U.S. Army; Tara, an intensive care nurse and captain in the National Guard; and Amy, a seventh grade teacher. The McCaffreys also have two grandchildren, Michael and Jack.